Expect the Most

Provide the Best

How High Expectations, Outstanding Instruction, & Curricular Innovations Help All Students Succeed

Robert L. Green, Ph.D.

George White, M.A., Kevin K. Green, Ph.D., Bradley Carl, Ph.D.

FOR ADDITIONAL COPIES, OF THIS TITLE AND OTHER PROFESSIONAL BOOKS, AT A 25% DISCOUNT, CONTACT: GWEN PAQUETTE GPAQUETTE@SCHOLASTIC.COM

SCHOLASTIC

New York • Toronto • London • Auckland • Sydney
Mexico City • New Delhi • Hong Kong • Buenos Aires

Dedication

This book is dedicated to all students who are struggling academically; who, too often, face the challenges of poverty in both urban and rural areas of America. This book is also dedicated to teachers, school administrators, and parents of the young people we serve. Let's expect the most and provide the best!

Acknowledgments

Special thanks to George White for his leadership and the overall development of the manuscript, which included research, writing, and editing. Also, special thanks to Kevin Green and Bradley Carl for their research and writing on significant expectations issues.

I'm also grateful to my wife, Lettie, for her never-ending support of my work. In addition, I want to express my appreciation for my other two sons, Vince and Kurt Green, because they have also been advocates for the high expectations required to help low-income and minority youth achieve academically.

I want to acknowledge Greg Worrell, president of the Scholastic Classroom & Community Group, and Lois Bridges, our Scholastic editor. Greg encouraged me to pursue new research on the power expectations. Lois was supportive, encouraging, and always responsive. I have worked with numerous editors over these many years and Lois ranks Number 1. Her high intellect and editorial strengths are appreciated. And copy and production editor Danny Miller and designer Sarah Morrow were both indispensable members of the team.

Much of this publication is based on research and insights from my years of service as a consultant for many urban school districts—the Dallas Independent School District and the Las Vegas, Nevada-based Clark County School District among them. My understanding of the nexus between high expectations and academic achievement has been shaped by my engagement with school administrators, parents, university researchers and—most of all—students from pre–K through high school.

The most important influences on my life-long work in urban education were my parents, Thomas and Alberta Green, because they held high expectations for their nine children, pushed us to succeed academically, and urged us to always reach out to help others.

Cover Designer: Brian LaRossa
Editor: Lois Bridges
Copy/Production Editor: Danny Miller
Interior Designer: Sarah Morrow
Copyright © 2014 by Robert L. Green
All rights reserved. Published by Scholastic Inc.
Printed in the U.S.A.
ISBN: 978-0-545-58885-0

CONTENTS

Foreword

by Ambassador Andrew J. Young

As a former mayor, congressman, and U.N. ambassador, I have seen how education can advance individuals, communities, and countries. Sadly, many American students are falling behind in the academic achievement race.

American teens scored below the international average in math and were only average in science and reading compared to the dozens of other countries that participated in the most recent Program for International Student Assessment (PISA). Thirty-five countries outperformed the U.S. in mathematics. Among the most economically advanced countries, the U.S. slipped from 14th to 20th place in reading and dropped from 17th to 25th in science.

Asian countries outperform the rest of the world in the latest annual PISA survey, which evaluates the knowledge and skills of the world's 15-year-olds. A report on the results cites the reasons for the Asian academic advance:

> The survey reveals several features of the best education systems. Top performers, notably in Asia, place great emphasis on selecting and training teachers, and they encourage them to work together and prioritize investment in teacher quality, not classroom sizes. They also set clear targets and give teachers autonomy in the classroom to achieve them.
>
> Children whose parents have high expectations perform better: they tend to try harder, have more confidence in their own ability, and are more motivated to learn.

To be sure, expectations are a key to academic achievement, and no one has done more to document this fact than Robert L. Green, who has written and edited many publications on the power of high standards. In *Expect the Most—Provide the Best*, Dr. Green and his co-authors—George White, Kevin Green, and Bradley Carl—cite the latest and best approaches to helping parents and teachers raise their standards in a way that also lifts the expectations and performance of students.

For example, co-author George White, an award-winning journalist and education policy analyst, provides cutting-edge strategies for engaging parents in education. He also identifies promising American initiatives in knowledge-sharing among teachers, a practice that has enabled Asian educators to excel.

Other major changes in education and academic expectations—those born of innovation—are also explored in *Expect the Most*. For example, digital technology is expanding our capacity to teach and learn. Dr. Kevin Green, a computer vision scientist who has won awards as a math teacher, identifies some of the more promising Web-based resources and software applications. He also explores the growing understanding of the relationship between literacy and the capacity to learn science, technology, engineering, and math (STEM).

Meanwhile, as federal programs such as No Child Left Behind and Race to the Top require more accountability in public schools, the expectations for the roles of school principals are also changing. Dr. Bradley Carl, a leader in research on school accountability systems, analyzes the evolving standards that are the basis for evaluating teachers and school administrators.

Finally, *Expect the Most* reflects Dr. Robert L. Green's extensive experience and scholarship on the expectations factor in student achievement and includes his insights on how to improve professional development programs for educators.

This book—a must-read for teachers, school administrators, and parents—is a primer on the innovation required to get American students back in the academic race.

Harness the Power of Expectations

At the beginning of the school year, two Harvard researchers, Robert Rosenthal and Lenore Jacobson, working in a public elementary school in a predominantly lower-income community, gave the students an intelligence test they called "The Harvard Test of Inflected Acquisition." They provided the teachers with precise information about the test's ability to determine intelligence quotients (IQs). What's more, they led teachers to believe that the test could also identify those students— "academic spurters"—who would make rapid, above-average intellectual progress over the course of the new school year. This prediction of success was not tied in any way to the students' current academic standing. Rosenthal and Jacobson then gave the teachers the names of those students who, on the basis of the test, were expected to demonstrate high academic success. In truth, the researchers had randomly selected the names from class lists. Contrary to what they had told the teachers, the test did not identify academic spurters. "Any differences between these children and the rest of the class existed only in the heads of the teachers" (Newman & Smith, 1999).

At the end of the school year, Rosenthal and Jacobson administered a second intelligence test. The results—now well-known in the annals of educational research—

are astonishing. The students who had been identified as "academic spurters" showed, on average, an increase of more than 12 points on their IQ scores, compared to an increase of 8 points among the rest of the students. The differences were even larger in the early grades. Almost half of first- and second-grade spurters achieved an IQ increase of 20 points or more.

And, not surprisingly, the teachers' own assessment of these students showed a similar surge. Not only did the teachers give the spurters higher reading grades, but also their highest regard. They viewed their "gifted" students as friendlier and better behaved, more intellectually curious, and with overall greater chances for future success. And the spurters responded accordingly. All that positive teacher attention and encouragement added up to increased student self-esteem. The students felt special and more capable and produced work that reflected their increased self-confidence.

The Rosenthal-Jacobson study—captured in their book *Pygmalion in the Classroom* (1968)—is a perfect example of a self-fulfilling prophecy. When we believe something to be true and act as though it is true, through the strength of our convictions and actions, we may, in fact, make it true. As Deborah Stipek, former Dean of Education at Stanford University, explains:

> *The term "self-fulfilling prophecy" is apt because once an expectation develops, even if it is wrong, people behave as if the belief were true. By behaving this way, they can actually cause their expectations to be fulfilled. Self-fulfilling prophecies occur only if the original expectation was erroneous and a change was brought about in the student's behavior as a consequence of the expectation (2011).*

The danger, of course, is that negative expectations can become self-fulfilling prophecies as well. Abundant research documents the fact that it's primarily our diverse students who suffer the negative consequences of low teacher expectations. As summarized by New York University researcher Pedro Noguera in the February 2012 issue of *Phi Delta Kappan*:

> *On all of the indicators of academic achievement, educational attainment, and school success, African American and Latino males are noticeably distinguished from other segments of the American population by their consistent clustering at the bottom (Schott, 2010). With few exceptions, the dismal patterns exist in urban, suburban, and rural school districts throughout the United States. Nationally, African American and Latino males are more likely than any other*

groups to be suspended and expelled from school (Fergus & Noguera, 2010). In most American cities, dropout rates for African American and Latino males are well above 50%, and they're less likely to enroll in or graduate from college than any other group (Schott, 2010).

African American and Latino males are more likely to be classified as mentally retarded or to be identified as suffering from a learning disability and placed in special education (Losen & Orfield, 2002). They're more likely to be absent from gifted and talented programs, Advanced Placement and honors courses, and international baccalaureate programs (Noguera, 2008). Even class privilege and the material benefits that accompany it fail to inoculate Black males from low academic performance. When compared to their White peers, middle-class African American and Latino males lag significantly in grade-point average and on standardized tests.

The impact of expectations on learning is well-documented in educational psychology. Studies have shown that the expectations others have for us influence the way we view ourselves. Moreover, how we view ourselves affects our own expectations. In turn, our expectations have a significant impact on our performance.

Consider the work of Carol Dweck, a Stanford University psychologist. Writing in her book *Mindset: The New Psychology of Success* (2006), Dweck introduces her readers to two mental constructs: fixed mindset and growth mindset. As the labels suggest, people with a fixed mindset believe they come into the world with a fixed amount of intellectual firepower. They accept failure as an inevitable reflection of their cognitive limitations. People with a growth mindset, on the other hand, refuse to be limited by real or imagined deficiencies of any sort. They believe that with enough hard work, perseverance, and practice, success is inevitable. Our book expands on methods that help teachers raise their standards in a way that also lifts the expectations of students.

Higher expectations are not an amorphous goal. As a result of the accountability movement in public education, it has recently become a factor in how teachers and school principals are evaluated. Chapter 5 explains how the expectations factor is measured in these evaluations.

THE ROLE OF FAMILIES, PRINCIPALS, AND PROFESSIONAL DEVELOPMENT

The power of harnessing expectations is not confined to the classroom. Access to exemplary professional development by families, principals, and teachers is of immeasurable value in establishing high expectations for both students and for the adults who strive to help them.

Families

Research makes clear the pivotal role of family engagement on academic achievement (Scholastic FACE Research Compendium, 2013; Redding, et al., 2011; Henderson, Mapp, et al., 2007). Regarding early readers, for example, researchers documented the value of parental involvement in children's literacy learning (Teale, 1987; Needlman, et al., 2006). Dolores Durkin (1966) was among the first to find that early readers tended to have parents or family members who read aloud to the child, took time to interact with the child, and provided reading and writing materials. Since Durkin's seminal research, many others have demonstrated similar results including, most notably, Neuman & Celano (2006); Snow & Juel (2005).

Increasingly, classroom teachers are recognizing the potential impact of parental and family involvement. In 2011, Scholastic released the results of an important survey it conducted in partnership with the Bill and Melinda Gates Foundation. In the survey, 98% of teachers said more family involvement and support would have a strong impact on academic achievement. Also, in the same survey, the importance of family involvement was cited more than any other factor. If educators are to successfully engage parents and families, teachers and school administrators must raise their expectations of their abilities to do so. The expectations of parents regarding their ability to make a difference must also be raised. In addition, teachers must learn more about the effective strategies for engaging parents and families. This book addresses these challenges.

Principals

Meanwhile, as the Common Core State Standards and Race to the Top require more accountability in public schools, the expectations for the roles of school principals are also changing. Principals were once expected to focus primarily on managerial duties. Today, effective principals analyze data to drive successful instruction, develop public relations systems to engage and inform the community, and conduct research on trends and best practices. *Expect the Most* explains these changes and provides a primer on effective school administration practices based on these higher expectations.

Professional Development

We have long known that it's the quality of the teaching in our classrooms that makes the difference for all students. Indeed, students with access to outstanding teachers often make more than a year's growth academically. Accordingly, the standards for professional development programs for educators are also rising. Professional training is essential if teachers and school administrators are to hone and advance their skills. However, recent studies suggest that much of the training is not effective. This book reviews these studies and underlines the importance of systems that evaluate training outcomes. Professional development makes a difference; top-notch professional development makes the biggest difference of all.

DIGITAL INNOVATIONS

Other major changes in education and academic expectations—those born of innovation—are also explored in *Expect the Most*. For example, digital technology is expanding our capacity to teach and learn. Increasingly, school districts are expected to take advantage of this technology and this generation of more tech-savvy students is prepared for the change. Chapters 7 and 8 provide a primer on some of the more promising Web-based resources and software applications. Chapter 8 also explores the educational potential of mobile phone technology. The book also shows how we can expand what we expect from school districts as more of them adopt digital technology for knowledge-sharing across district lines.

Expect the Most also explores the growing understanding of the relationship between literacy and the capacity to learn math, science, engineering, and technology. As this connection becomes clearer, we can raise our expectations of students' ability to learn—what is for many—daunting study courses.

For example, there has been a campaign to turn the acronym STEM—science, technology, engineering, and mathematics—into STEAM by adding the visual "arts." The movement stems from the recognition that visual thinking—recognizing and forming patterns, modeling, and manipulative skills learned by using tools, pens, and brushes—have applications in STEM-related subjects.

STREAM!

So we know that STEM stands for Science Technology Engineering and Mathematics, and we get STEAM by adding the Arts. But just adding the arts isn't enough; we need to add the thinking skills embodied in reading and writing—hence the latest iteration, STREAM! Like any other art form, writing embodies the entire range of thinking tools required for any creative endeavor. To be an effective writer, one must observe, create abstracts from key information, recognize and create patterns, and use analogies and metaphors. These skills are also applicable to math. As for science and engineering, learning those subjects requires a capacity to understand a vocabulary related to the disciplines. To master these subjects, one must master reading. *Expect the Most* also shows us how some school districts are learning that they can raise expectations and achievement in STEM-related subjects by adopting project-based learning approaches that challenge and excite students.

LET'S EXPECT THE MOST—AND PROVIDE THE BEST—FOR ALL STUDENTS

Expect the Most—Provide the Best combines the expertise and experience of scholars and analysts who have explored these emerging pathways to academic achievement. It reflects Dr. Robert L. Green's extensive experience and scholarship on many factors related to student achievement—the impact of expectations among them—and it incorporates George White's expertise on community outreach, research analysis, and parental engagement. This book also includes Dr. Kevin K. Green's insights on STEM, STEAM, and STREAM. In addition, it provides Dr. Bradley Carl's analyses of the evolving standards—the expectations factor among them—that are the basis for evaluating teachers and school administrators.

Expect the Most also includes modules on best practices and brief profiles of high achievers and innovators—advocates of the high expectations required to help all learners succeed and close the academic achievement gap.

Chapter 1

The Achievement Gap and Why It Matters

The best-selling book *The Other Wes Moore* is a compelling story of how education can dramatically affect life outcomes. The book profiles two boys living in the same city who happened to have the same name. One grew up to be a Rhodes Scholar, decorated combat veteran, White House Fellow, and business leader. The other is serving a life sentence in prison for felony murder. The statistics surrounding the relationship between educational achievement and life outcomes are not always as stark as in the case of the two Wes Moores—but they do tend to be clear and compelling.

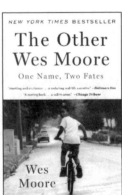

Consider the link between education and income. According to a recent Georgetown University study (2011) based on U.S. government statistics, individuals with a bachelor's degree make 84% more over a lifetime than those with only a high school diploma. The study's projections on education levels and future employability are stunning. It estimates that by 2018, 63% of U.S. jobs will require some form of post-secondary education or training. "Unfortunately," says the report, "we are woefully unprepared for this reality as a nation. Today, approximately 41% of adults have a college degree in America."

Moreover, the lack of education often does lead to the kinds of devastating outcomes illustrated in *The Other Wes Moore*. The socio-economic and life consequences of failing to complete high school are startling, especially for people of color. Consider the fate of many black men in this country. A *New York Times* (2012) article based on a report published by the Russell Sage Foundation included the following: "Among male high school dropouts born between 1975 and 1979, 68% of blacks (compared with 28% of whites) had been imprisoned at some point by 2009, and 37% of blacks (compared with 12% of whites) were incarcerated that year."

As you can see, the stakes are extremely high. Let's review some of the most recent data on academic achievement.

ACHIEVEMENT GAP SUMMARY: NAEP AND HIGH SCHOOL COMPLETION RATES

Performance data from the National Assessment of Educational Progress (NAEP), often referred to as the "Nation's Report Card," provide a commonly used measure of achievement gaps that exist between different student subgroups. The main NAEP assessment has been administered to a representative sample of 4th and 8th grade students in reading and mathematics for several decades, allowing for longitudinal comparisons of performance that include a focus on achievement gaps by racial/ethnic group and gender.

In Grade 4 math, the graph and table below show that the average scale score among black and Hispanic public school students (both males and females) increased between 2000 and 2011, but black-white and Hispanic-white performance gaps closed only slightly since white students both made gains *and* started at higher performance levels.

Grade 4 Math Scale Scores by Subgroup, 2000-2011, National Public Schools

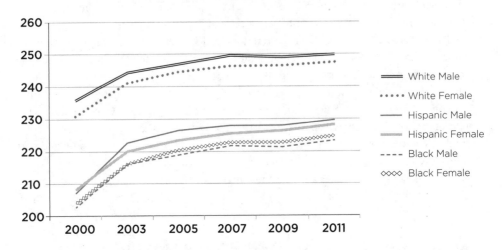

Table A: Grade 4 NAEP Math Scale Scores by Subgroup, Selected Years 2000-2011

	2000	2003	2005	2007	2009	2011	Change
White Male	236	244	247	249	249	250	+14
White Female	231	241	244	246	246	248	+17
Hispanic Male	207	223	227	228	228	230	+23
Hispanic Female	208	220	223	226	226	228	+20
Black Male	202	216	219	221	221	223	+21
Black Female	204	216	220	223	223	225	+21

In Grade 8 math, black and Hispanic students again made substantial gains over the past decade that were nearly twice those of white students, but achievement gaps again remained large due to higher starting points for whites.

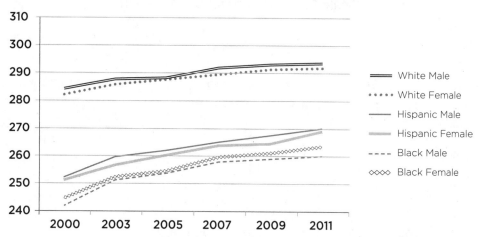

NAEP National Public Grade 8 Math
Scale Score by Subgroup, 2000–2011

Table B: Grade 8 NAEP Math Scale Scores by Subgroup, Selected Years 2000-2011

	2000	2003	2005	2007	2009	2011	Change
White Male	284	287	288	292	293	293	+9
White Female	282	286	287	289	291	292	+10
Hispanic Male	252	260	262	265	267	270	+18
Hispanic Female	251	257	260	264	264	269	+18
Black Male	242	251	254	258	259	260	+18
Black Female	244	252	255	260	261	264	+19

Gains in NAEP 4th grade reading scores among all student subgroups were considerably smaller than in math, with black and Hispanic students' growth again outpacing that of whites. Both the black-white and Hispanic-white gaps remained in the 20–25 point range, however.

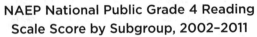

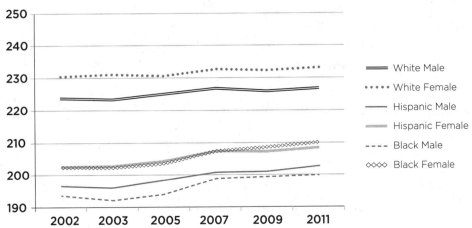

Table C: Grade 4 NAEP Reading Scale Scores by Subgroup, Selected Years 2000-2011

	2000	2003	2005	2007	2009	2011	Change
White Male	224	223	225	227	226	227	+3
White Female	231	231	231	233	232	233	+2
Hispanic Male	197	196	199	201	201	203	+6
Hispanic Female	202	203	204	207	207	208	+6
Black Male	193	192	194	199	199	200	+6
Black Female	202	202	204	207	209	210	+8

Grade 8 reading scores followed much the same pattern, with larger gains between 2000 and 2011 for Hispanic and black students (both male and female) than were observed for white students, with achievement gaps closing slightly, but remaining in the 20-25 point range, due to white students starting at higher performance levels.

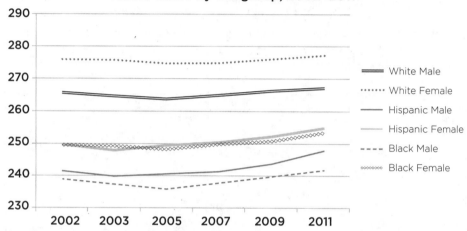

NAEP National Public Grade 8 Reading Scale Score by Subgroup, 2002–2011

Table D: Grade 8 NAEP Reading Scale Scores by Subgroup, Selected Years 2000-2011

	2000	2003	2005	2007	2009	2011	Change
White Male	266	265	264	265	267	267	+1
White Female	276	276	275	275	276	277	+1
Hispanic Male	241	240	241	241	243	248	+6
Hispanic Female	249	248	249	250	252	255	+5
Black Male	239	238	236	238	240	242	+3
Black Female	250	249	248	250	251	253	+4

In addition to results from the NAEP, which compares performance of students in reading and math at grades 4 and 8 over time, there is also a "long-term" version of NAEP that tracks the performance of U.S. students at ages 9, 13, and 17. Tracking performance by student age, rather than grade level, is noteworthy when considering urban student populations, which tend to have higher shares of students who have been retained at grade level. Many urban districts have particularly high retention rates among 9th graders, such that the age span of 9th graders ranges from 14 (a typical first-time 9th grader) to 17 (a student who has been a 9th grader for three years without earning enough credits to be promoted to grade 10). Accordingly, long-term NAEP results for 17-year-olds include students enrolled across the entire spectrum of grades 9–12.

VOICES FROM THE FIELD

Researcher Bradley Carl

Working With Teachers on Data Literacy

Understanding school accountability systems and measures of school and principal effectiveness—important topics in current educational policy discussions—often requires an understanding of statistical concepts that many teachers have not had reason to review in a long time, if ever.

Keeping up on best practices in differentiated instruction and sound classroom management, after all, are understandably more urgent for most teachers. However, it is often the case that knowledge of a few key statistical concepts goes a long way in helping educators understand and feel more comfortable with the accountability systems that are increasingly being used to judge their performance. Those who help develop these accountability and teacher evaluation systems—including myself—should continue to seek ways to explain technical concepts in an easily-understood manner.

Long-term NAEP results generally display similar trends to those observed for the main NAEP—specifically, that black and Hispanic students have made substantial gains that are much greater than those of their white peers while remaining far behind white students' overall performance levels. Comparing the performance of 17-year-olds may be particularly insightful in this regard. Black 17-year-olds' reading scores increased 26 points between 1980 and 2012 (from 243 to 269) while Hispanic students' scores jumped 13 points (from 261 to 274). White students' performance over the same 32-year span was nearly flat (293 in 1980 and 295 in 2012), while remaining 20-25 points higher than for black and Hispanic students. In math, black 17-year-olds' scores jumped 16 points between 1982 and 2012 (from 272 to 288) while Hispanic students' scores increased by 17 points (from 277 to 294). Over the same 30-year time frame, white students' scores went up by a more modest 10 points—from 304 to 314—but remained 20 points higher than both black and Hispanic students.

High school and college completion rates provide another very important and useful metric for tracking achievement gaps over time. Data from the U.S. Census Bureau's Current Population Survey summarized below in Table E show that the percentage of all adults ages 25 and over who have completed high school has risen steadily over the past 40+ years, to the point where nearly 9 in 10 adults have attained this level of education. High school completion rates have risen among all racial/ethnic subgroups and both genders. (However, the percentage of Hispanics who have completed high school remains substantially below the rates for both whites and blacks.) In Table F, which shows the percentage of adults age 25+ who have completed four years of college (without necessarily having earned a degree), we observe that gains have again been made by all subgroups—although notable black-white and Hispanic-white gaps remain. In contrast to whites, where the percentage of males who have completed four years of college remains above the rate for females, among both blacks and Hispanics it is females who have higher college completion rates.

What implications do gaps in educational attainment have for earnings? Data from the Current Population Survey summarized below in Table G show that those who fail to earn a high school diploma can expect to earn, on average, approximately $20,000 annually (and slightly less for black and Hispanic workers). This is approximately two-thirds of what will be earned by those with a high school diploma, half that of someone who earns an associates' degree and one-third that of someone who earns a bachelor's degree.

Table E: High School Completion Rates (Age 25 and Older) by Subgroup, Selected Years

YEAR	ALL RACES			WHITE			BLACK			ASIAN			HISPANIC		
	Total	Male	Female	Total	Male	Female	Total	Male	Female	Total	Male	Female	Total	Male	Female
2012	87.6%	87.3%	88.0%	88.1%	87.6%	88.5%	85.0%	84.3%	85.5%	88.9%	90.4%	87.6%	65.0%	64.0%	66.0%
2005	85.2%	84.9%	85.5%	85.8%	85.2%	86.2%	81.1%	81.0%	81.2%	87.6%	90.4%	85.2%	58.5%	57.9%	59.1%
2000	84.1%	84.2%	84.0%	84.9%	84.8%	85.0%	78.5%	78.7%	78.3%	(NA)	(NA)	(NA)	57.0%	56.6%	57.5%
1990	77.6%	77.7%	77.5%	79.1%	79.1%	79.0%	66.2%	65.8%	66.5%	(NA)	(NA)	(NA)	50.8%	50.3%	51.3%
1980	68.6%	69.2%	68.1%	70.5%	71.0%	70.1%	51.2%	51.1%	51.3%	(NA)	(NA)	(NA)	45.3%	46.4%	44.1%
1970	55.2%	55.0%	55.4%	57.4%	57.2%	57.6%	33.7%	32.4%	34.8%	(NA)	(NA)	(NA)	(NA)	(NA)	(NA)

Source: U.S. Census Bureau, Current Population Survey

Table F: College Completion (Four Years) Rates (Age 25 and Older) by Subgroup, Selected Years

YEAR	ALL RACES			WHITE			BLACK			ASIAN			HISPANIC		
	Total	Male	Female	Total	Male	Female	Total	Male	Female	Total	Male	Female	Total	Male	Female
2012	30.9%	31.4%	30.6%	31.3%	31.9%	30.8%	21.2%	19.2%	22.9%	51.0%	53.7%	48.8%	14.5%	13.3%	15.8%
2005	27.7%	28.9%	26.5%	28.1%	29.4%	26.8%	17.6%	16.0%	18.8%	50.2%	54.0%	46.8%	12.0%	11.8%	12.1%
2000	25.6%	27.8%	23.6%	26.1%	28.5%	23.9%	16.5%	16.3%	16.7%	(NA)	(NA)	(NA)	10.6%	10.7%	10.6%
1990	21.3%	24.4%	18.4%	22.0%	25.3%	19.0%	11.3%	11.9%	10.8%	(NA)	(NA)	(NA)	9.2%	9.8%	8.7%
1980	17.0%	20.9%	13.6%	17.8%	22.1%	14.0%	7.9%	7.7%	8.1%	(NA)	(NA)	(NA)	7.9%	9.7%	6.2%
1970	11.0%	14.1%	8.2%	11.6%	15.0%	8.6%	4.5%	4.6%	4.4%	(NA)	(NA)	(NA)	(NA)	(NA)	(NA)

Source: U.S. Census Bureau, Current Population Survey

Table G: Mean 2009 Earnings (in dollars) by Educational Attainment Level, Selected Subgroups

	MEAN EARNINGS BY LEVEL OF HIGHEST DEGREE (DOLLARS)							
	Not a high school graduate	High school graduate only	Some college, no degree	Associate's	Bachelor's	Master's	Professional	Doctorate
ALL:	20,241	30,627	32,295	39,771	56,665	73,738	127,803	103,054
Male	23,036	35,468	39,204	47,572	69,479	90,964	150,310	114,347
Female	15,514	24,304	25,340	33,432	43,589	58,534	89,897	83,708
WHITE:	20,457	31,429	33,119	40,632	57,762	73,771	127,942	104,533
Male	23,353	36,418	40,352	48,521	71,286	91,776	149,149	115,497
Female	15,187	24,615	25,537	33,996	43,309	58,036	89,526	85,682
BLACK:	18,936	26,970	29,129	33,734	47,799	60,067	102,328	82,510
Male	21,828	30,723	33,969	41,142	55,655	68,890	n/a	n/a
Female	15,644	22,964	25,433	29,464	42,587	54,523	n/a	n/a
HISPANIC:	19,816	25,998	29,836	33,783	49,017	71,322	79,228	88,435
Male	21,588	28,908	35,089	38,768	58,570	80,737	n/a	89,956
Female	16,170	21,473	24,281	29,785	39,566	61,843	n/a	n/a

Source: U.S. Census Bureau, Current Population Survey (www.census.gov/compendia/statab/cats/education/educational_attainment.html)

So, what does all this mean with regard to where we go from here? Let's consider the context of inequality in education. Ideally, our American education system was designed to make it possible for all—regardless of income, race, and ethnicity—to achieve and move up the socio-economic ladder. It has often been called the "great equalizer." However, in the mid-1960s, a U.S. government-sponsored report, *Equality of Educational Opportunity*, said that the biggest influence on student achievement was the socio-economic status of the communities in which schools were located (Coleman, 1966).

This was not exactly a shocking revelation. We've always known that wealthy communities provide more resources for their schools. For example, Susan Neuman's seminal research reminds us that while "children from middle-income neighborhoods are likely to be deluged with a wide variety of reading materials," children from poor neighborhoods go without: their families can't afford books, their public libraries, if they are open at all, have drastically reduced hours of operation; school libraries are in "serious disrepair"(and increasingly without school librarians), and preschools in poor neighborhoods are largely without any books at all (p. 21). There is currently a debate over the level of impact financial resources has on academic achievement, but no one would argue that the learning environments in rich neighborhoods and most schools in poor communities are very different. Consider this report from an in *Education Week* (April 12, 2013) on educational inequality:

> *Take for example, the conditions in a typical low-income, mostly minority community: expectations for all students are low, students get As for doing mediocre work, the curriculum is not challenging, classrooms are constantly disrupted, teachers have a hard time maintaining order, students who strive for academic excellence are ostracized by their peers, and few go to college.*
>
> *In a wealthy school district serving mostly students from well-to-do families, all is reversed: expectations are high, classroom discipline is not a problem, students are paying attention; they have to work for their As and are not ostracized by their peers for doing well in their classes. The curriculum is challenging and designed to put all students on a track that will get a great majority of them into selective colleges.*

While there are always exceptions, children in low-income communities are more likely to attend substandard schools than children who attend school in a community of means. The great divide described in that report and in government studies help account for an achievement gap that has a significant impact on life outcomes. However, there is an important factor—one referenced in many studies on scholastic excellence—that can help counter the bad learning conditions in poor neighborhoods and make a major difference despite resource disparities. We will explore, explain, and document how high expectations can empower communities to boost academic achievement.

VOICES FROM THE FIELD

Professor Gary Orfield

Co-Director, Civil Rights Project at UCLA

Access to High-Quality Teaching: Disparities

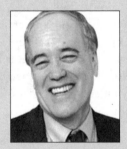

Professor Gary Orfield was co-founder and director of the Harvard Civil Rights Project and is now co-director of the Civil Rights Project at UCLA. He has been a research leader on education policy as it relates to equal opportunity in America. Here are some of his statements on disparities in access to high-quality teachers.

- "Segregated black and Latino schools have less-prepared teachers . . . ."

- "We now have a society where 44% of our public school children are non-white and our two largest minority populations, Latinos and African Americans, are more segregated than they have been since the death of Martin Luther King more than forty years ago. Schools remain highly unequal, sometimes in terms of dollars and very frequently in terms of teachers . . . and other key aspects of schooling."

- "Experienced teachers . . . stay in stable integrated neighborhoods, but are much more likely to leave in the face of resegregation." (Orfield 2009)

Professor Ronald Ferguson

Director, Achievement Gap Initiative at Harvard University

Quality Teaching and Student Achievement

Ronald F. Ferguson is Senior Lecturer in Education and Public Policy at the Harvard Graduate School of Education. He also serves as faculty co-chair and director of the Achievement Gap Initiative at Harvard University. He has taught at Harvard since 1983, focusing on education and economic development. Much of his research and writing over the past decade have focused on racial achievement gaps. Some of that work has centered on the impact of quality  teaching on academic achievement. Ferguson outlines seven "strategic propositions" that characterize those school districts that serve as academically effective learning havens for students:

- **Leadership That Combines Passion With Competence**
  Superintendents, principals, other administrators, and even lead teachers effectively cultivate not only a sense of urgency but also a sense of possibility, built on demonstrated expertise among people in key positions and their commitment to continuous improvement.

- **Clear, Shared Conceptions of Effective Instruction**
  The district identifies key ideas concerning effective instructional and supervisory practice, and works to establish them as a "common language" for approaching instructional improvement.

- **Streamlined and Coherent Curriculum**
  The district purposefully selects curriculum materials and places some restrictions on school and teacher autonomy in curriculum decisions. The district also provides tools (including technology) and professional development to support classroom-level delivery of specific curricula.

- **Organizational Structures and Personnel That Embody Capacity to Teach and Motivate Adults**
  The district maintains routines and structures within which adult educators engage teachers and administrators in continuous improvement of instructional and supervisory practices. Coaching, observing, and sharing make it difficult for individuals to avoid the change process, and the push for adaptive change spurs resisters to leave their comfort zones or eventually depart from the district.

- **Patient but Tough Accountability**
  The district develops tools and routines for monitoring teaching practices and learning outcomes, targeting assistance where needed, and sometimes replacing teachers or administrators who fail to improve.

- **Data-Driven Decision-Making and Transparency**
  Teachers and administrators analyze student performance for individual students and summarize data by grade level, special status, race/ethnicity, and gender. The district publicizes strategic goals for raising achievement levels and reducing gaps and tracks progress in visible ways. Administrators identify, examine, and often emulate practices from successful schools.

- **Community Involvement and Resources**
  The district engages a broad range of stakeholders, including school board members, local businesses, and parents, to do their parts toward achieving well-formulated strategic goals.

WHERE DO WE GO FROM HERE: TRANSITIONS TO HIGHER STANDARDS

As a nation, well inside the 21st century, we're reexamining what it means to educate our young people. What are the skills our students need to thrive in our new globalized era, the so-called Knowledge Age, in which information and ideas lie at the heart of civic, technological, environmental, and economic well-being and growth. In our increasingly complex world with its exploding information such essential cognitive strategies as analysis, interpretation, problem solving, and reasoning are more important than ever.

Developing "Literate Capacities"

Whether you live in a state that is implementing the Common Core State Standards or you are following your own state's higher standards, all aim to help students become fully literate young people—confident learners who can read critically, ask essential questions, follow a line of inquiry, articulate their own ideas, and, in general, enjoy the life of the mind robust literacy makes possible. We might define literate capacities as follows:

- **Demonstrate independence.** Students are able to comprehend and critique a wide range of text types and genres, pinpoint the key message, request clarification, and ask relevant questions.

- **Build strong content knowledge.** Students engage with rich content through wide-ranging quality texts; in the process, they learn to read purposefully, often led by their own essential questions.

- **Respond to varying demands of audience.** Students become text- and audience-sensitive, understanding that different texts arrive in different formats and serve different purposes.

- **Comprehend as well as critique.** In this era of print and multimedia bombardment, teachers recognize that their ultimate aim is to help their students become critical readers, so they not only understand the message but also can question its assumptions, relevance, and soundness.

- **Value evidence.** Again, with the explosion of new information, students need to learn how to back up what they say and write with evidence.

- **Use technology and digital media strategically and capably.** Technology offers a universe of learning, but students need guidance in how to conduct efficient, productive online searches and then integrate what they learn into other media. Students also need to have a sense of what technology can and cannot do—what are its limitations?

- **Come to understand other perspectives and cultures.** Reading in general and literature in particular have always offered the promise of transcendence, of an opportunity to experience other lives, perspectives, values, and beliefs.

Increasingly, educators look to new, higher academic standards to help their students develop the essential thinking skills needed to address the multi-faceted literacies of our new century. Preparing our students for the rigors and challenges of 21st-century living is the challenge that fuels the work of thoughtful educators. And ever-mindful of the increasing pressure educators face as they work to address the new standards, we have attempted to draw together some of research, the experts, and the resources that will help you create and implement a strategic plan as you transition to higher standards.

Chapter 2

The Expectations Factor in Student Achievement

The impact of expectations on student achievement has been documented for decades (Green, 1987; Berndt and Miller, 1990; Stipek, 2002; Noguera, 2012; Bromberg & Theokas, 2013). The role of teachers in setting high standards has been the focus of significant research. Much of that research has focused on African American students (Wood, Kaplan and McLoyd, 2007). For example, Ronald Ferguson, a Harvard professor who has assessed the impact of expectations, concluded that teachers' standards and behaviors help sustain—and perhaps expand—test score gaps (Ferguson, 2003).

Expectations, the standards or the bar we set for others, can be a major factor in effort and in outcomes. Teachers with high expectations will seek to have students achieve those standards. Students will make an effort to meet those standards if they have high expectations for themselves. Conversely, low expectations discourage effort and achievement.

Teachers play a pivotal role across all seven propositions outlined by Ferguson (see p. 24) and, indeed, when teachers establish both *rigorous and relevant* expectations (Daggett, 2014) students typically thrive; sadly, when teachers don't expect enough, the opposite is also true.

Research on student achievement and classroom standards has identified the following as indicators that teachers or administrators have low expectations of their students:

- Rarely ask specific questions.

- Don't insist that homework be turned in on time.

- Lesson plans are poorly prepared or lack rigor.

- Homework is not corrected and returned to students in a timely manner.

- Display angry disposition.

- Accept poor or incorrect answers from students.

- Advance few students of color into advanced or STEM courses (science, technology, engineering, and mathematics); students from poor communities are disproportionately steered into special education classes or schools.

- Disproportionate number of students from one racial or ethnic group are suspended or expelled.

CASE STUDIES ON THE IMPACT OF HIGHER EXPECTATIONS

Often, the best way to understand what works in schools—to understand how schools and districts can create a *culture of excellence*—is to look deeply at schools and districts that excel at providing children with an exemplary education. In the section that follows, we showcase both outstanding districts and individual schools that foster a culture of excellence.

Resource Spotlight

MODEL SCHOOL CONFERENCE

For a firsthand explanation of schools that work, consider attending the Model Schools Conference, which features the nation's highest-performing schools, cutting-edge educational leaders, and the tools and resources needed to drive excellence and improve student learning and engagement. Model Schools are the nation's most innovative schools with proven successful practices for increasing student achievement. Outstanding educators from a cross section of model elementary, middle, and high schools present a rich array of approaches to delivering world-class education.

For more information, see International Center for Leadership in Education.

Case Study: Cumberland County Schools, North Carolina

Cumberland County Schools (CCS) is the fifth largest school system in the state and 78th in the nation, serving over 53,000 students and 87 schools in southeastern North Carolina. The racial composition of the student population is 44.91% African American, 1.69% Asian, 10.93% Hispanic, 1.92% Native American, 33.78% White, and 6.46% Other. The federal government is the largest employer in the county followed by CCS.

CCS serves a low-income district. More than 56% of students meet poverty standards for the federal meal subsidy program. Cumberland County is the largest low-wealth county in North Carolina. Despite the lack of financial resources, students at schools within CCS are excelling. The turnaround at one of the county's schools was cited in a May 27, 2011 article in the FayObserver:

> *Test scores at E.E. Smith High School were so dismal in 2006 that a Superior Court judge threatened to restructure the school and remove its principal unless at least 55% of students passed end-of-course tests.*
>
> *The following year, a new principal with new ideas stepped in at E. E. Smith, demanding high expectations from teachers and students alike.*
>
> *Two years later, 89.3% of white E. E. Smith students passed end-of-course tests, along with 83% of black students. The achievement gap fell from 26.7 percentage points in 2007–08 to 6.3 last year.*
>
> *High expectations and a willingness to relate to students on a personal level are keys to success . . . principals say.*

This culture of high expectations is mandated by the Cumberland County School District. It was explained by CCS School Superintendent Frank Till in his 2013 report for AdvancED (Till, 2013), a global association that provides accreditation, program evaluations and research for school districts in the U.S. and abroad:

> *All students can achieve at high levels, and it is our responsibility to ensure ALL students graduate ready for college or career—and ALL MEANS ALL. Our school system believes there are no boundaries to student success.*

However, expectations are not the only factor in the school district's success. In his report to AdvancED (2013), Superintendent Till revealed the other factors—collaboration, student evaluation regimens, and achievement improvement systems.

Collaboration is necessary on every level to arrive at the decisions needed to serve our students. We believe in speaking and acting with "one voice." At the school level, the Student Services Team (SST) meets to determine a plan to meet individual student needs. Each school has a School Improvement Team (SIT) made up of staff, students, and parents that develop the school improvement plan and make decisions for school implementation. Attendance area schools meet in Vertical Teams to align school and community activities and provide support for each other ensuring collaborative competition. Instructional Council, Job-A-like groups, Advisory Teams, and Task Force Committees provide input into system-wide decisions.

We believe that decisions are supported when a collaborative approach to decision-making is implemented. Our school system developed and uses the CCS ASPIRE Model in some decision-making processes. The cycler steps for continuous improvement of the ASPIRE process are Analyze data, Seek input, Plan, Implement the plan, Revise or review, and Evaluate.

Support is provided to all schools from the various CCS departments. School Support Directors visit schools daily to monitor the needs of schools by reviewing data, budget decisions, personnel concerns, facility needs, professional development needs, and program implementation issues. Resources, services, and support are directed to the schools based on data and dialogue with principals and other staff within the school. The levels of support are outlined in the Differentiated Support and Accountability Framework and vary based on school performance.

High-quality instruction is the expectation in all CCS classrooms. High-quality instruction is defined in CCS as reflecting the Six Characteristics of a Great Classroom. These characteristics include:

1. positive emotional climate

2. organized lessons

3. engaged learners

4. meaningful learning

5. continuous monitoring and feedback

6. academic rigor with high expectations for all students

The high-quality instructional environments of CCS provide opportunities for students to think critically, collaborate, communicate, and develop creativity. Students must be prepared for success in their future workplace and for success in life.

CCS believes in an ongoing process of instructional monitoring and analyzing data to improve student achievement. Appropriate ongoing assessment and monitoring techniques are used to evaluate learning and adjust instruction. Data gained from assessments are reviewed at the classroom, school, and district level. Trends in the data direct instructional practices to ensure individual students' continued growth and achievement.

Case Study: Excellence Boys Charter School, New York

Individualized assessments, time-on-task systems, and high expectations are also part of the learning culture at Excellence Boys Charter School, located in Brooklyn's Bedford-Stuyvesant community. High expectations are embedded in the name of the school—"Excellence." Standards are also part of other terminology at the school, which serves about 400 boys in grades K–8. For example, teachers refer to students as "scholars" and homerooms bear university names.

Jabali Sawicki, principal at the Excellence school, cites those standards and the results:

> Excellence Boys has unapologetically high expectations for each of our scholars for both academics and behavior. We cultivate in our young men the knowledge, skills, and character necessary to succeed academically, embrace responsibility, and become honorable citizens and courageous leaders. In 2009, in grade four, 90% of students passed reading exams at Advanced or Proficient levels; in grade five, 100% of students passed math exams at Advanced and Proficient levels—placing Excellence among the top schools in New York City (Educational Testing Service, 2011).

Higher expectations are an essential first step to higher achievement. However, the school has also created a learning culture and support systems to help generate high achievement. Let's review some important components and the related the standards espoused on the schools' website.

Culture of Learning

[Our] students expect excellence from one another. This means that it is "cool" for boys to be smart, curious scholars who show excitement for school and enthusiasm for learning. Free from social pressures and stereotypes, students at Excellence Boys help each other succeed and feel safe taking responsible academic and personal risks. There are no limits to life's possibilities for our students.

. . . Each week ends with a Friday Community Meeting in both the Elementary and Middle Academies. Each Community Meeting features student accomplishments and reinforces the values that are celebrated at Excellence Boys. Classes perform memorized poems related to school values, individual students present knowledge they acquired during the week, teachers highlight exceptional academic work, and the Spirit Stick is presented to the student who best exemplified the spirit of Excellence Boys. This scholar then has the honor and responsibility of carrying the Spirit Stick throughout the following week, serving as a role model to other students.

Maximizing Time-on-Task

At Excellence Boys, we give our students every possible chance to learn. A longer school day from 7:30 AM to 4:00 PM, a longer school year, small class-sizes, and homework every day for every student result in more time on task for students. In addition to intensive language arts and math instruction each day, we also provide after-school tutoring, a Saturday Tutoring Academy, and summer-school remediation. High expectations for our students are meaningless if we cannot provide the resources that they need to fulfill those expectations.

Approach to Literacy and Math

The most important factor determining success in school is a child's ability to read. The strongest indicator of future college-attendance is a child's coursework in mathematics.

Excellence Boys Charter School's academic program emphasizes these two disciplines. Every K–4 Elementary Academy student has at least three periods of language arts instruction (phonics, reading comprehension, writing, and either the Waterford computer-based literacy program [K–1] or independent work [2–3]), and math class each day, as well as social studies and science. Our Middle Academy scholars have 55-minute periods each day dedicated to our core subjects, including Reading, Writing, Math Problem Solving, Math Procedures, History, and Science (Sawicki, 2013).

Case Study: Eagle Academy, New York

Standards are also the key to success at schools launched and managed by the Eagle Academy Foundation in New York City. The Eagle Academy schools are often cited as model venues of black male academic achievement. The academy states that "academic rigor and high expectations flow beyond the traditional school hours to the mandatory extended-day and Saturday Institute programs, which include workshops for parents, life-skills training, and remedial services for our students." Launched in the Bronx in 2004 to address the failure and dropout rates of black boys, Eagle now has middle and high schools in Brooklyn, Queens, and in a community near Newark, New Jersey. About 95% of Eagle students continue on to college.

How do they do it? It starts with expectations embedded in a student contract. The contract sets clear standards for behavior, personal accountability, and personal responsibility. Each student signs the contract, which is read at the opening day convocation as a reaffirmation of the student's commitment to himself and the school's mission.

Results generate demand. The Eagle Academy for Young Men opened in the fall of 2004. From there, Eagle developed into a full 4-year high school and moved to its current state-of-the-art flagship facility in 2009. During the 2011–2012 school year, the school opened its doors for its first 6th grade class and now provides instruction in grades 6 through 12.

The Eagle Academy for Young Men has also expanded beyond its initial Bronx roots by opening three additional schools in Ocean Hill/Brownsville Brooklyn, South Jamaica Queens, and Newark, New Jersey. All schools are supported by the Eagle Academy Foundation, which was created as a result of the initial investment of a group of educators, parents, community leaders, and corporate partners, led by the One Hundred Black Men, Inc., a national association of African American professionals with chapters in major cities.

Case Study: Urban Prep, Chicago

Other all-male public charter schools have also had success by emphasizing high expectations. For example, Chicago's Urban Prep made national news in 2010 when it announced that 100% of its black male seniors had enrolled in college. Dr. Jawanza Kunjufu, the school's founder, stressed the impact of teacher expectations in an interview in the *Journal of African American Males in Education* (Johnson, 2011). He said his approach includes "raising teacher expectations, increasing time on task, understanding that children have different learning styles, [and] making curriculum more culturally relevant."

The curriculum "difference" at Urban Prep and the Eagle Academies is a greater emphasis on the achievements of ancient African civilizations and the triumphs of African Americans. Kunjufu referenced similarities in approach to these daunting situations in an interview with the *Journal of African American Males in Education* (Kunjufu, 2011).

> [In] my hometown (Chicago), we are all very proud of the work being doing at the Urban Prep and in New York at Eagle Academies. And while there are several positive factors that these schools use in their outstanding quest toward creating beautiful and meaningful experiences for African American males, I must say that these schools demonstrate and show that if you have high expectations, good classroom management, and a commitment toward understanding the various learning styles of males, then students will strive and surpass even our own high expectations.
>
> The company that I started (African American Images, Inc.) developed Self-Esteem Through Culture Academic Excellence (SETCLAE), a culturally relevant curriculum for students and teachers. We have seen tremendous growth with many charter schools that have adopted and applied SETCLAE principles at their respective schools. Since 1988, test scores have improved over 40% and the longitudinal data clearly demonstrates that culturally relevant activities and curricular approaches really do work best with and for our children.

Case Study: Eleanor Roosevelt High School, Prince George's County, Maryland

Some traditional public schools are also combining curricular innovations with high expectations. For example, Eleanor Roosevelt High School in Prince

George's County, Maryland, has very high goals. It has a stated commitment to having all of its nearly 2,800 students ready for college by the time they graduate. A report posted on the website of the College Board, the company that administers the AP and SAT tests, says students entering the school "know what they're getting into . . . High expectations are described to students and families, and big dreams are encouraged."

About 67% of students at Roosevelt are African American. The high school divides students into smaller learning communities, such as academies for science and technology, health and human services, and business and law. The College Board recently recognized Roosevelt as one of the nation's best high schools at producing successful black AP test-takers. Roosevelt is a two-time winner of the U.S. Department of Education's National Blue Ribbon School of Excellence, an award that honors schools that have achieved high levels of performance or significant improvements, with emphasis on schools serving disadvantaged students.

Roosevelt's success also underlines the value of curricula specialization, which attracts students with high expectations and great interest in specific studies. Specifically, the school offers a highly challenging four-year curriculum that provides college-level academic experiences in science, math, and technology. Here are some samples of course descriptions that can be found on the Roosevelt website (Roosevelt, 2013).

Web Page Design (1/2 Tech Ed Credit)

This is an introductory semester course to the fast growing industry of website design and development. This course will introduce web design concepts and skills, vocabulary, software applications, evaluation techniques, and related social and ethical issues. This project-based course will provide students with a solid understanding of the entire website development process.

Introduction to Business (1 Credit)

This full-year course unlocks the mysteries of business operations and what impact they have on individual lives. It gives students experience and confidence in making responsible business decisions. This course features consumer buying, income taxes, banking, budgets, credit, saving and investing, insurance, stocks and bonds, owning and marketing a business, and much more.

Business Law (1/2 Credit)

This semester course is a study of the legal rights and responsibilities of adults and minors in civil and criminal actions. Emphasis is placed on laws as applied to ethics, contracts, sales, court systems, employment, and personal business transactions. The concepts and skills will be useful in future business and personal situations. This course is a good foundation for students who plan to major in business in college.

Business Management (1/2 Credit)

This semester course is a motivational guide to becoming a successful business owner, board chairperson, or company president. It is designed to give students insight on the qualities necessary for effective leadership and career success.

Case Study: Houston Independent School District, Houston, Texas

The Houston Independent School District (HISD) also aims to generate academic excellence by adopting higher standards. Apollo is a groundbreaking program designed to improve the academic achievement of students in twenty HISD "priority" schools and to create models for excellent teaching and learning. With help from Harvard Professor Roland Fryer, a champion of high expectations, Apollo was launched in four high schools and five middle schools at the start of the 2010–11 school year.

The program is guided by five broad strategies: (1) effective teachers and principals at every school; (2) more instructional time; (3) data-driven instruction; (4) high-dosage tutoring; and (5) a culture of high expectations. The district set the bar high by establishing the following expectations:

- 100% of students performing on or above grade level
- 100% of students taking at least one college-level course
- 100% graduation rate
- 95% attendance rate for students and staff
- 100% of students accepted to a four-year college or university

The college-bound standard for all (100%) Apollo students is central to the "No Excuses" philosophy that Apollo has adopted from the Knowledge Is Power Program (KIPP), which operates more than 100 schools nationwide. That standard is also a criterion for selecting principals and teacher.

All of the principals and 169 of the teachers at the original Apollo schools were replaced with faculty applicants who successfully passed screenings designed to identify principals and teachers most committed to the "No Excuses" philosophy. Many of the teachers selected also had a record of producing high grades and high achievement.

Teaching applicants were also required to commit to Apollo's "turnaround" schools for at least two years. In addition, Apollo selected teachers believed to be most likely to provide more feedback in the classroom.

Apollo is also hiring hundreds of tutors, "math and reading fellows" who receive $20,000 a year, health benefits, and a performance-based bonus of $5,000. The fellows provide an hour of tutoring to students each school day.

The school day at Apollo secondary schools was lengthened by one hour four days a week, and the school year was lengthened by ten days. Apollo elementary schools offer Saturday school and after-school tutorials.

In addition, the high expectations code was formalized. Clear expectations were set for school leaders and families were asked to sign contracts committing to the program. Student achievement performance goals were set for each school and principals were held accountable for meeting them.

The mechanism for meeting the goals is "data-driven" instruction that requires the schools to analyze student performance regularly and to use that data to tailor lessons to address individual needs.

Eleven Houston elementary schools were added to the Apollo program during the 2011–2012 academic year. Initial results from the original nine—the five middle schools and four high schools—have been promising. Harvard researchers determined that Apollo 20 schools improved their achievement in math by 0.276 standard deviations.

WHERE DO WE GO FROM HERE? TRUST AND A DYNAMIC LEARNING FRAME

Holding high expectations for our students begins with trust—trusting ourselves to be respectful of and responsive toward every student—and trusting, as well, that every student is a capable learner. Stanford researcher Carol Dweck (2006) reminds us of the importance of framing our work with our students around a *growth mindset*—believing that all students are able to grow, change, and become confident and successful learners.

In his book *Opening Minds* (2013), language researcher Peter Johnston explores similar territory. He refers to a dynamic learning frame versus a fixed one. The differences between the two are pronounced and, as they unfold in school and beyond, they can make a huge difference in the life of a student. As their names imply, a *fixed performance frame* is informed by a belief that every human being is born into the world with a set cache of intelligence and ability governed by a predetermined limit. It's not possible to go over your limit. Those with a *dynamic learning frame*, on the other hand, see the world as one intriguing challenge after another. The more you try, the more you learn, and the more capable you become. There's no such thing as failure because every experience, including the less successful ones, is an opportunity for growth.

Johnston compares and contrasts the two learning frames:

Fixed-Performance Beliefs and Dynamic-Learning Beliefs	
Fixed Performance Frame	**Dynamic Learning Frame**
People have fixed traits, such as smartness, intelligence, and personality that they cannot change.	The more you learn, the smarter you get. You can change your mind, your smartness, and who you become.
Learning happens quickly for smart people, so trying hard is not valued; if you have to try hard, you probably aren't smart.	Learning takes time and effort, so trying hard is valued.
The most important information is whether one is successful. It shows who is smart and more valuable. How one succeeds is irrelevant. (Cheating and lying can be justifiable routes to success.)	The most important information is how someone did (or could do) something, because that's what we can learn from.
The goal is to look as smart as you can.	The goal is to learn as much as you can.
Frequent success without trying is an indicator of one's (fixed) ability and value.	Frequent success without trying hard indicates choosing activities that are too easy to learn from.
Problems/challenges/errors are indicators of one's intellectual ability.	Problems/challenges/errors are to be expected if a person is taking on challenge—which is valued (even experts/authors make mistakes).
Challenging and novel activities are risky/stressful.	Challenging and novel activities are engaging.
Competition is important and success requires ability and a competitive focus. Seeking help is evidence of one's intellectual inadequacy.	Collaboration is important and success requires it, along with interest and efforts to comprehend. Seeking help is sensible after exhausting one's own resources.
Greater competence means being smarter and therefore better (and more valuable) than others, and potentially having power over others.	Greater competence means being able to take on new challenges and greater opportunity to help others.

Chapter 3

Expectations, Race, and Ethnicity

Across the nation, some teachers are lowering the expectations of students of color, sometimes without even realizing it. Consider this exchange, which occurred recently at a Detroit middle school.

The instructor, a math teacher, is asking each of the students about their career objectives. One African American male student raises his hand.

"I want to be a math teacher," he says.

"You're not smart enough to be a math teacher," says the instructor. "You should be a truck driver."

An education consultant is in the classroom, and he notices that the boy is visibly crestfallen. After the class, the consultant visits with the student and learns that the boy's father is a truck driver, something the teacher obviously knew. In a bid to off-set the teacher's remarks, the consultant tells the student that truck driving is honorable work but that he should aim higher.

"If you decide to be involved in trucking," says the consultant, "you don't have to be a driver. You can be a trucking business owner."

In most situations, teachers who lower students' expectations do it subconsciously, but there are also more blatant, conscious actions such as the teacher comment at that Detroit middle school. To be sure, there is a large body of research that demonstrates that many teachers have low expectations of black and brown students in urban schools and that, in turn, often leads to students lowering their own standards.

Research also shows that these low expectations result in lower academic black student achievement (see Wildhagen, 2012; Green, 2002, 1996 and 1977). Harvard Professor Ronald Ferguson (2003, 1998) concluded that teachers' perceptions, standards, and behaviors sustain and probably help expand the test score gap between black and white students. Ogbu (2003) and Fordham (1988) also studied the issue and suggested that low expectations on the part of teachers contribute to the creation of anti-intellectual identities among African American students, an attitude that equates academic achievement negatively as "acting white." Indeed, this culture—in which academic achievement is considered as neither possible nor desirable—has been documented by other scholars (Wildhagen 2012; Hill, 1998; Green, 1998a, 1997; Kotlowitz, 1991).

Conversely, cultural attitudes about the athletic capabilities of black students—the expectations of teachers, school coaches, and the students themselves—are very high and that is one reason so many African Americans have excelled in this area. In one elementary school, for example, a group of teachers encouraged a consultant to witness the jump-roping skills of a ten-year-old black boy. "He can skip rope like [boxer] Floyd Mayweather," one teacher exclaimed. The other teachers said they referred to the child as "Mayweather." However, when the consultant asked the teachers about the boy's academic progress, they were all unaware of his reading and math scores.

Other research has documented the impact of expectations on other students of color. Terrill and Mark (2000) found that teachers have lower expectations for Native Americans in rural schools compared to their attitudes toward whites. In another study—one involving Latino students—Armendariz (2001) found that bias against Latinos is institutionalized in public schools. He concluded that the norms, behaviors, and values of white teachers are manifested in low expectations for Latinos and a devaluing of the skills, knowledge, and self-concepts that these students learn in their homes and communities.

Psychologists and education researchers have concluded that the expectations of non-white students are commonly lowered by "tracking" them into lower level classes, which makes them feel less intelligent. Tracking is assigning students to comparable courses based on degree of difficulty—basic, honors, or college prep among them. This, according to Stanford psychologist Claude M. Steele (1998, 1997, 1995), is "stereotype vulnerability." All students experience anxieties over possible academic failure; however, members of non-white groups experience more difficulty because of stereotypical notions about how well they can and will perform. The students understand that they are not expected to do well and—as a result—they do not.

"Intelligence plus character—
that is the goal of true education."

—Martin Luther King, Jr. (1947). The Purpose of Education. *The Maroon Tiger* (Morehouse College campus newspaper), Atlanta, Georgia

Research has demonstrated that the students' environment can also help induce lower expectations. For example, Kozol (1991) contended that the low expectations of poor and minority students stems in part from their awareness of substandard facilities within their schools. They equate, he said, deteriorating buildings, dirty floors and toilets, and poor plumbing with the larger society's low expectations. Other scholars have documented the impact of a correlation between teachers' standards and job satisfaction levels with the physical conditions of the school as it relates to student expectations (Green, 2002; Lippmann, Burns & MacArthur, 1996; Wang & Gordon, 1994; Taylor, 1994). In recent years, many states have been forced to cut funding for school maintenance because their tax revenues have dropped during recessionary years.

All of these findings are alarming because urban and minority students need high expectations to counteract other potential negative pre-determinants such as crumbling neighborhoods, poverty, and crime.

Robert's Reflections

[As we prepared this section on race, expectations, and achievement, I reflected on the role of my parents as creators of high academic expectations for me and my eight siblings. Here's an excerpt from *At the Crossroads of Fear and Freedom: A Memoir on the Fight for Social and Educational Justice*]:

My father only finished the fourth grade, and my mother was educated until the ninth grade. However, they valued education and made it clear to us that educated blacks would have opportunities. They made sure we completed our homework, ensured that we had supplies and books—and not just the textbooks required by schools. In addition, they made it clear that they had high expectations and that we should also adopt high standards.

. . . I thought of a 1982 article on the Green clan in *Crisis* magazine, published by the NAACP. The article summarized the Green family belief in the power of education and our dedication to learning and social justice. I found that article, written by Chester Higgins, and began to re-read it.

Robert Green's four sisters

"The Green family of Michigan State University puts a premium on learning and social involvement.

"Robert L. Green remembers his father's hardheaded philosophy: go to school and worship the Lord. Through the years it has stuck with him and eight brothers and sisters and their offspring, more than 35 in all, who have gone on to attain, or are in the process of attaining, undergraduate and advanced college degrees."

I paused at that point and smiled because the article had been published 20 years ago and the number of my nieces and nephews with degrees is much higher now. In all, my family and the families of my brothers and sisters had obtained 109 degrees as of 2012—8 PhDs, 8 medical degrees and 3 M.B.A.s among them. I am "Uncle Bob" to men and women who have obtained advanced degrees at major universities, including Michigan State, *continued . . .*

Yale Law School, Harvard and Columbia Law Schools, University of Michigan, Notre Dame, and the University of Colorado. My eldest brother, Havious, had eight daughters and they all obtained Ph.D.s or M.D.s.

My part in this legacy is my three sons—Robert Vincent, who has B.A. and a law degree; Kurt, with an M.B.A. and a B.A., and Kevin, with Ph.D., M.S. and B.S. degrees in electrical engineering. My wife Lettie, a Registered Nurse, began reading to them in their infant years. Their early acquisition of literacy skills has helped them become outstanding in the fields of Law, Finance, and Engineering.

(above) My wife Lettie
(left) Our three sons Robert Vincent, Kurt, and Kevin

HIGH EXPECTATIONS AND POVERTY

Like race and ethnicity, poverty can be a factor in academic performance. However, being poor—like being black or Latino—is not a barrier to achievement.

The real barriers to learning are these:

- Indifference

- Rejection

- Poor instruction

- Low expectations for student success

Hunger and Neglect

Hunger, low self-esteem, and truancy can stem from poverty or parental neglect. There are two types of poverty. One is the lack of financial resources. The other is a poverty of the spirit, which often stems from the more widely recognized lack of economic resources. The lack of strength and stamina that poverty and poor nutrition can cause must be addressed immediately; a teacher can be motivated, prepared and skillful; but a student cannot learn if he or she is hungry.

Under the federal Title One program, the children of families with low incomes can qualify for free breakfast or a free or reduced-cost lunch. However, those meals are not provided on weekends. Observant teachers can and should identify the students who are the most food-deprived. Throughout the nation, teachers can and do address the hunger barrier by getting the permission of the principal to put excess food from the federally funded school pantries into the backpacks of needy students on Fridays before they return home for the weekend. This is an informal practice that helps students who are victims of neglect or extreme poverty.

Hunger is not always physically apparent and some students—out of shame—will not tell teachers they are hungry. However, students often act out by misbehaving when they are hungry or become uncharacteristically quiet and withdrawn when they are distracted by hunger. Teachers should investigate anomalous behavior by privately talking to students to determine the root cause of problems.

Conversely, obesity can sometimes also be a sign of poverty because families that cannot afford to buy more nutritious food will over-consume more fattening processed food, carbohydrates, and sugar. In other situations, some families—those without automobiles—live in poor communities devoid of supermarkets and dominated by small stores that don't sell fresh produce.

Obesity can lead to many serious health problems—diabetes, heart disease, and strokes among them. This is not just a health problem for our children; it's also a learning problem. Studies have shown that inadequate consumption of key food groups deprives children of essential nutrients necessary for optimal cognitive function. For example, iron deficiency has been linked to shortened attention span, fatigue, and difficulty concentrating. Also, low protein intake has been associated with low academic achievement.

Studies have also shown that physical activity is an outlet for releasing tension and anxiety and facilitating emotional stability, which makes learning easier. According to the Centers for Disease Control and Prevention, children need at least one hour of exercise per day. However, many parents in poor communities do not allow their children to play or participate in sports outside because they live in high-crime neighborhoods.

To be sure, teachers are on the front lines and have opportunities to identify possible learning problems related to the lack of nutritious food and exercise. Traditionally, educators have not been expected to address learning barriers related to nutrition and fitness. Slowly, that is beginning to change as educators realize that it will be more difficult to raise expectations and achievement if these problems are not addressed.

Teachers, school principals, and administrators in some school districts are now taking steps to deal with nutrition and fitness impediments. For example, Matt Kelley Elementary, a school in a low-income community in Las Vegas, recently retained Lucille Young, a Robert L. Green & Associates wellness consultant who will be advising the school on nutrition and will be leading more structured exercise sessions for students.

While nutrition and fitness-related learning problems can be difficult to determine, other signs of poverty are very apparent. Worn-out clothing or shoes can be among those signs but can also be an indicator of neglect if, for example, there are also hygiene problems and apparel is dirty. Of course, parental neglect and abuse occurs in all economic classes. However, 85% of the states that report statistics on child abuse and neglect cite parental substance abuse and poverty as the top two factors.

Regardless of the income level, chronic and persistent bad hygiene and lack of grooming should be addressed to help the student and eliminate a possible classroom distraction. In those situations, teachers should report the problem to the principal or school counselor so that contact with parents can be initiated. In the most extreme situations involving unresponsive parents or guardians, school administrators may have to file a report with the local child protective services office.

Signs of neglect should be a red flag for a teacher. Neglected or abused children will often need more emotional and academic support from teachers.

Poverty of the Spirit

Poverty of the spirit can also have an impact on academic achievement. For example, negative self-esteem can be a side effect of impoverishment. Teachers can address this condition by reminding students that they have talent, worth, and values. To do this effectively, teachers must believe in the power of high expectations.

However, students in need of food, better guardianship, or the empowerment of high expectations, cannot have those needs adequately met if they are frequently absent from school. Several studies indicate a high correlation between poverty and chronic truancy, 20 or more absences from school during a school year.

The teacher should notify principals about students with truancy problems. The teacher should give those students more attention so they don't fall behind, with a focus on their reading and math capabilities. Teachers should not form negative attitudes about the parents of children who are truant or of those who show signs of hunger or neglect because educators need to be able to communicate with parents and encourage them to take more of an interest in their children's academic progress.

WHERE DO WE GO FROM HERE? REASON TO HOPE

One of my books, *The Urban Challenge—Poverty and Race*, was published in 1977. Unfortunately, many of the problems cited in the book—determinants of life prospects such as education, poverty, and housing—have not been solved (Green, 1977). However, considering the growing interest in the connection between expectations and student achievement—evident in the Common Core State Standards, a refined understanding of the essential role of student engagement, and the rise of such initiatives as Oakland Unified School District's African American Male Achievement—I am more hopeful than ever that we can close achievement gaps.

Chapter 4

Effective Teachers: Their Characteristics, Skills, and Practices

High expectations are an essential factor in student achievement. Effective teachers create high standards and develop strategies that help ensure that students embrace those expectations. The best teachers are committed to their own continual professional development understanding that it enhances their ability to raise expectations and achievement. Effective teachers understand the power of expectations, summarized below:

- Expectations that others have for us affect the way in which we view ourselves.
- The way we view ourselves affects our own expectations for ourselves.
- The expectations we hold for ourselves impact our performance and influence the nature and the quality of the lives we live.

CHARACTERISTICS OF EFFECTIVE TEACHERS

- **Effective teachers are optimistic and caring.** Effective teachers see students as individuals and want to be seen the same way. Such teachers are engaging people who demonstrate positive feelings.

- **Effective teachers believe in their ability to help students achieve.** Effective teachers believe that all students can and will learn in their classroom. They know that if they use effective strategies and motivation, students will excel.

- **Effective teachers enjoy their work.** If teachers enjoy seeing students raise their achievement levels, they are more motivated to help them excel.

- **Effective teachers appreciate and celebrate diversity in the classroom.** Our student populations are increasingly diverse, and our best teachers want to address the "diversity gaps" between teachers and students.

SKILLS OF EFFECTIVE TEACHERS

- **Effective teachers know how to develop excellent instruction plans.** They are able to plan for adequate instruction time, make smooth transitions to different topics, and pace instruction to ensure they engage students in challenging subjects.

- **Effective teachers have the ability to make learning fun.** They are able to design instruction in a way that challenges, engages, and rewards students. They realize that the ability to make the learning process exciting is a key to success.

- **Effective teachers can accurately gauge the progress and needs of their students.** With that capacity, teachers can set appropriate standards and expectations for individual students and tailor instruction accordingly.

PRACTICES OF EFFECTIVE TEACHERS

With input over the past two decades from principals, teachers, and instructional coaches around the country, we developed a list of important practices that make teachers effective in the classroom. Green's research and consulting partners—including contributors to this book—have refined and narrowed the list to the following 13 as most important.

- Effective teachers maintain an overall atmosphere (verbal and non-verbal) of general encouragement and support for the learning process of all students—and not just when students provide the correct lesson-related response to a classroom question. They generate a supportive, positive, and challenging atmosphere in the classroom. They act as a major resource of information and support to students.

- Effective teachers will get to know parents or guardians of the children in their classrooms.

- Effective teachers maintain an orderly environment that is safe, structured, and comfortable. They create a sense that the classroom is a place to concentrate on the learning at hand, rather than on immediate anxieties and distracting events at home or in the neighborhood.

- Effective teachers not only have high expectations but also set clear standards of attainable academic and behavioral performance, and hold students to them.

- Effective teachers carefully think, plan, and make decisions to ensure strategic teaching.

- Effective teachers give students adequate time to formulate answers when called upon. "Wait time" is used to cultivate good responses.

- Effective teachers react to student responses with praise at the appropriate time and in the appropriate amount. Praise is directed and specific, not general, stereotyped, or single-worded.

- Effective teachers use significant amounts of positive non-verbal behavior such as smiling, nodding positively, looking students directly in the eye, leaning forward, and encouraging more than one direct response.

- Effective teachers design learning activities to be challenging, engaging, relevant, and directed to student motivations. They emphasize the process of learning and its excitement as a quest.

- Effective teachers place primary stress on academic achievement and do not settle for solely social or other non-academic goals, such as success in school athletics.

- Effective teachers see the good in each student and expect excellence.

- Effective teachers help struggling students develop good work habits.

- Effective teachers understand the relationship between health, nutrition, and learning.

Rebecca Lynn Mieliwocki

Luther Burbank Middle School, 2012 National Teacher of the Year

Rebecca Mieliwocki is a 7th grade English teacher at Luther Burbank Middle School, which houses 1100 students in grades 6–8. She has been teaching for 14 years and has spent 9 years in her current position. Rebecca holds a Bachelor of Arts in Speech Communication from California Polytechnic State University and her Professional Clear Credential in Secondary English Education from California State University Northridge. She is the 2005 California League of Middle Schools Educator of the Year for Southern California, a 2009 PTA Honorary Service Award Winner, and a BTSA mentor, and has also served as a teacher expert for CSUN College of Education Panel titled "The ABC's of IEPs."

A child of two veteran public school teachers, Rebecca initially shied away from becoming a teacher, but she soon realized there is "no nobler profession" than teaching. Her own K-12 teachers serve as her heroes, and she models her teaching style on the example they set for her. She works hard to provide her students with exciting and dynamic lessons that are both educational and amusing.

Rebecca says, "Students learn best when they have the most enthusiastic, engaged teachers possible." She believes strongly in the importance of good teacher preparation programs, continuous support and collaboration opportunities for veteran teachers, and a strong school leadership team to guide and drive achievement. She values the teaching profession as a sought-after career and one that can transform our nation for the better. She says, "I firmly believe that teachers must be held accountable for their students' success, from helping them meet personal or school-wide learning goals to achieving on district and state level assessments. Our students are our future, so we, their teachers, must do our best to inspire them and guide them to greatness" (CCSSO, 2012).

AWARENESS: A KEY TO RAISING ACHIEVEMENT

The characteristics, skills, and practices we've discussed are not enough if teachers are not conscious of the needs of all students. The following are awareness factors that are keys to success.

- **Practice cultural awareness**. Understand that the culture and background of a student is not an excuse for failure; we're obligated to believe in and engage all students.

- **Address the needs of at–risk students.** We must identify our at-risk students. Many have relatives who were low-achievers or dropouts. Challenging family situations are not excuses for low expectations and low achievement. Many may have also previously had teachers who held low expectations for their success. Knowledgeable and effective teachers make these students feel wanted and help them excel in potentially difficult subjects, especially reading and math.

- **Monitor our own classroom demeanor.** If we are upbeat, students will sense that disposition and often respond accordingly. If we are in an angry mood or frustrated, students will sense that, and many will not respond well to instruction. Teachers should always remain calm and engaging.

- **Realize our limitations but help students who need special counseling.** Effective teachers are not expected to be social workers, but they should know when to refer students to school counselors, social workers, and/or psychologists.

VOICES FROM THE FIELD

Larry Cuban

Meeting and Exceeding Student Expectations of Teachers: A Way to Achieve "Good" Teaching

Go into most public school classrooms and you see a sign, usually in the front of the classroom, listing what the teacher expects of students in classroom behavior.

> **CLASS RULES**
> - Be Prompt
> - Be Prepared
> - Be Positive
> - Be Productive
> - Be Polite

   Experienced teachers advise new ones to make these rules explicit and enforce them from day one. Folk wisdom among veteran teachers is that expecting this behavior and equitably acting on the rules will lead to an orderly classroom. So most new and experienced teachers, believing this advice and wanting a well-managed classroom, list classroom rules. Some adventurous teachers have students construct the rules since they are well aware of acceptable classroom behavior from previous teachers.

   In addition to behavior, what teachers expect of students academically influences achievement. Researchers have established that when teachers have high or low expectations of what their students can achieve—especially low-income and minority students—those expectations color what students do achieve (Good, 1987, 32–47). The point is that teacher expectations of student behavior and academic performance matter.

What is often missing from the advice given to teachers, however, is what goes on in students' heads as they see a new teacher (novice or veteran) for the first time. Students also have an informal list of what behaviors, knowledge, and skills they expect of their teachers. And just like teacher expectations, student expectations matter.

Expectancy theory, as *academics* call it, involves motivation and choice—if I expect something and I want it to happen, I will choose that action that best achieves what I want. And that is true of student motivation and choosing what to do (or not do) in a classroom or lesson.

Beginning in kindergarten (or preschool), over the years students develop views of what a "good" teacher and good teaching are. By the time, students are in high school, they have implicit models in their heads of who good teachers are and what they do in organizing and teaching a class.

By "good" teacher, most students mean one who mostly leads a teacher-centered, subject-driven academic class. The opposite of "good" is "bad." For students meeting teachers for the first time, "bad" means the teacher tries to be friends with students, uses techniques (e.g., abandoning the textbook, peer grading of quizzes) that are seldom used by other "good" teachers. They tolerate it when students misbehave and students ignore what they say. In short, "bad" teachers cannot maintain minimum order in the classroom.

None of this is meant to imply that students' pictures of "good" teachers are correct, only that students already have ideas of what they believe is institutionally "good" for them.

So if a novice teacher (or veteran who transfers to a different school) believes that students have blank slates when they meet each other for the first time, they are whistling the wrong tune. Let me give examples of student expectations of teachers that I have encountered over the years.

- "Good" teachers know more facts and concepts than students do about the subject.

- "Good" teachers answer student questions clearly and correctly.

- "Good" teachers take time to explain complicated content.

- "Good" teachers do not publicly humiliate students.

- "Good" teachers assign homework from the text.

- "Good" teachers clamp down on late-comers to class.

- "Good" teachers break up fights between students and protect weak students from being bullied.

- "Good" teachers do not permit students to copy from one another when expecting each student to do his or her work.

- "Good" teachers do not allow students to sleep in class.

For novices and veterans new to a school to ignore what students have learned about teachers and teaching from many years of sitting in classrooms is ultimately condescending since teachers are dismissing important student beliefs and knowledge. It also makes much harder the long-term task of developing strong relationships with the class as a whole and with individual students—both essential for learning to occur.

There is a catch, however, when new and veteran teachers meet student expectations. To do only what students expect is to be trapped by their traditional expectations of what a "good" teacher is. The tightrope act teachers have to negotiate is initially to meet what students expect—"good" teaching—then move students beyond those beliefs and begin reshaping their expectations of "good" teaching. Teachers need to get students to appreciate and learn from a far larger repertoire of classroom approaches and they need to develop the personal relationships with students that is essential for learning to occur.

So, the essence of what I offer is for new and veteran teachers meeting their students for the first time is straightforward: know what students expect of "good" teachers and teaching, meet those expectations, and then, once strong relationships have been formed with students, move beyond them so students can enlarge their picture of what "good" teachers and teaching are.

INSTITUTIONALIZED LOW EXPECTATIONS

Can low expectations be institutionalized throughout a school district system? This news columnist suggests that this is exactly what is happening in Florida.

Esther Cepeda

Lowered Student Expectations Is the Wrong Approach

When prospective educators go through training to prepare for teaching low-income, minority, or at-risk children, they learn how to empathize with their students' lives. They're taught to acknowledge environments lacking in resources, order, or stability and "meet" the students at their level before expecting them to learn as easily as other children do.

Yet rare are the educators who believe this enough to push such students toward their full academic potential. Instead, educators come up with misguided policies to go easy on groups of underperforming students, perpetuating the worst kind of disrespect—lowered expectations—on whole categories of children who are assumed to be less capable.

Disrespected, underestimated, and left behind is how you might imagine many Florida students and their parents felt about the new standards. The Southern Poverty Law Center filed a civil rights complaint against their state board of education's strategic plan, which sets less ambitious goals for black and Hispanic students than for white and Asian ones.

Approved last fall, the plan is designed to reduce below-grade-level performance by categorizing K-12 students into subgroups with adjusted goals for each. Where it goes astray is in expecting less of certain students based on their race.

The Florida Board of Education set the 2018 goal for reading at grade level at 90% for Asian students and 88% for white students, while expecting only 81% of Hispanic and 74% of black students to do so.

In math, 92% of Asian-American students and 86% of white students are expected to perform at grade level by 2018, but this is expected only of 74% of black students and 80% of Hispanic students.

I'm not suggesting that Florida's Board of Education is racist, but it seems as though they've bought into the victim narrative that so often permeates discussions about poverty.

Don't all students deserve the same optimistic belief in their potential?

Students do deserve the same optimistic belief in their potential. This practice in Florida is an indication that institutionalized low expectations based race and ethnicity continues.

WHERE DO WE GO FROM HERE?
PROFESSIONAL LEARNING FOR TEACHERS

We have long known that it's the quality of the teaching in our classrooms that makes the difference for all students. Indeed, students with access to outstanding teachers often make more than a year's growth academically in a single year. And new research suggests that an early start with a superb teacher may shape a student's chances for lifelong success (Chetty, 2011). In other words, access to an exemplary master teacher is the gift that keeps on giving.

What seems like simple common sense—that a teacher steeped in professional theory and practice is a more effective teacher—is backed by convincing research. Systematic and sustained professional development with embedded support improves student achievement—fostering engaged, active learning and improving standardized test scores: "Teachers who receive substantial professional development—an average of 49 hours a year—can boost their students' achievement by approximately 21 percentile points" (Yoon, et al. 2007).

While test scores are certainly a key indicator of student success, we strongly recommend that you look beyond just grades and tests and, instead, focuses on whether learners are equipped with the skills and knowledge they need to thrive in our complex and ever-changing world.

High-Quality Professional Development

High-quality professional development centers on student learning. The content of professional development can make the difference between enhancing teachers' competence and simply providing a forum for teachers to talk. The most useful professional development emphasizes active teaching, assessment, observation, and reflection rather than abstract discussions. Professional development that focuses on student learning and helps teachers develop the pedagogical skills to teach specific kinds of content has strong positive effects on practice.

What's more, professional collaboration lies at the heart of effective professional learning. Great things are possible when teachers are trusted and treated as professional educators, given the time and resources to work together, and supported through a range of professional structures, strategies, and solutions.

Research supports professional development that

- Deepens teachers' knowledge of content and how to teach it to students.
- Helps teachers understand how students learn specific content.
- Provides opportunities for active, hands-on learning.
- Enables teachers to acquire new knowledge, apply it to practice, and reflect on the results with colleagues.
- Links curriculum, assessment, and standards to professional learning and comprehensive school reform.
- Is collaborative and collegial.
- Is intensive and sustained over time.

Ultimately, as John Hattie (2009) reminds us, teachers must enter their classrooms determined to foster effort and engagement for every student. Teachers must regard themselves as change agents—people who can make an immense difference by believing that all students can learn and progress, that achievement for all is dynamic and possible—not static and fixed—and that all students, with enough hard work and perseverance, can not only succeed but also thrive (Dweck, 2006).

Chapter 5

Accountability, Administrators, and Parents

A substantial and growing body of educational research (see, for example, Rivkin, Hanushek, and Kain, 2005; Rockoff, 2004) confirms that teacher and principal quality are the most important school-based influences on student learning and have long-term impacts on students' success beyond K–12 schooling (Chetty, Friedman, & Rockoff, 2011). Accordingly, school districts, states, and the federal government have moved increasingly in recent years toward re-designing the human capital management systems that are used to recruit, hire, mentor, train, evaluate, and compensate their teachers and principals. At the federal level, this emphasis on improving teacher and principal quality is evident through major U.S. Department of Education policy initiatives that include state waivers from the Elementary and Secondary Education Act, the Race to the Top competitions, and the Teacher Incentive Fund (TIF) grant program.

THE EXPECTATIONS FACTOR IN TEACHER
AND PRINCIPAL EVALUATION SYSTEMS

In establishing new guidelines for evaluating the performance of teachers and principals, states and school districts have adopted models that include a combination of student outcome measures plus observations of teacher and principal practice (see Kane, McCaffrey, Miller, & Staiger, 2013; Mihaly, McCaffrey, Staiger, & Lockwood, 2013; Goe, Holdheide, & Miller, 2011). Observations of educator practice are conducted by trained evaluators using rubrics based on recognized standards for high-quality teaching and school leadership. For observing *teacher practice*, most states and districts are basing their new systems on standards developed by the Interstate Teacher Assessment and Support Consortium (InTASC), which has identified 10 Teaching Standards that discuss key characteristics of quality teaching. Teacher expectations for student performance are clearly embodied in InTASC Standard 2 (entitled "Learning Differences"), which lists the following as a Critical Attribute:

> *The teacher believes that all learners can achieve at high levels and persists in helping each learner reach his/her full potential (CCSSO, 2011: 13).*

As states have developed their own rubrics for evaluating teacher practice based on the InTASC standards, many have utilized Charlotte Danielson's *Framework for Teaching* or Framework (Danielson Group, 2013). Danielson is an internationally respected expert on teacher effectiveness who has advised education departments in the United States and abroad. Her Framework also features a significant emphasis on teachers having high expectations for student performance. The Framework consists of four main areas (called Domains) that define high-quality teaching, with each domain subdivided into smaller units known as Components and Elements. The importance of high expectations for student performance is clearly spelled out across the framework, most notably within Domain 2 (The Classroom Environment) and Component 2 (Establishing a Culture for Learning). In the overview of this component, Danielson notes that in "classrooms with robust cultures for learning, all students receive the message that although the work is challenging, they are capable of achieving it if they are prepared to work hard."

Teacher performance on the Danielson Framework is evaluated by rubrics which classify performance within each of the four domains as Unsatisfactory, Basic, Proficient, or Distinguished. Each level includes a summary of what teacher performance within that category looks like. Specifically, it is a set of "Critical Attributes" that describe key defining characteristics of each performance level and specific examples of behaviors and practices that trained evaluators look for when evaluating their teachers. The table below provides examples and a summary of how teachers' expectations for student performance are embodied in Domain 2a.

Performance Level	General Description	Critical Attributes	Possible Examples
UNSATISFACTORY	Medium to low expectations for student achievement are the norm, with high expectations for learning reserved for only one or two students.	Students use language incorrectly; the teacher does not correct them.	The teacher says to a student, "Why don't you try this easier problem?"
BASIC	High expectations for learning are reserved for those students thought to have a natural aptitude for the subject.	The teacher conveys high expectations for only some students.	The teacher does not encourage students who are struggling.
PROFICIENT	High expectations for both learning and hard work are the norm for most students.	The teacher conveys an expectation of high levels of student effort.	The teacher hands a paper back to a student, saying, "I know you can do a better job on this." The student accepts it without complaint.
DISTINGUISHED	The teacher conveys high expectations for learning for all students and insists on hard work.	Teacher conveys the satisfaction that accompanies a deep understanding of complex content.	A student asks the teacher for permission to redo a piece of work since she now sees how it could be strengthened.

For observing *principal practice*, most states are basing their new systems on standards for high quality school leadership developed by the Interstate School Leaders Licensure Consortium (ISLLC, 2008). ISLLC identifies six standards, each with several sub-categories (known as Functions) that spell out specific characteristics of high-quality school leadership. One example of a state-developed rubric based on the ISLLC standards is the Wisconsin Department of Public Instruction's Principal Evaluation Process Manual (DPI, 2013), which contains two broad categories (Domains) for principal practice that are broken down into five Components and 21 Elements.

The principal's role in creating and reinforcing high expectations for student achievement is clearly captured under 1.2.2 (Student Achievement Focus). Examples of each of the four performance categories (Unsatisfactory, Basic, Proficient, and Distinguished) and specific behaviors that evaluators look for under the Wisconsin rubric are as follows:

- **Unsatisfactory:** Principal tolerates poor student academic or behavioral performance or weak teacher focus on student achievement expectations.

- **Basic:** Principal sets expectations for student academics and behavior, but inconsistently holds students and teacher accountable to those expectations.

- **Proficient:** Principal sets expectations that teachers and staff contribute to clear, high, and demanding academic and behavior expectations for every student.

- **Distinguished:** Principal empowers teachers, staff, students, and other stakeholders to contribute to clear, high, and demanding academic and behavior expectations for every student that are reflected in the School Improvement Plan.

SCHOOL PRINCIPALS AND EXPECTATIONS

Research has shown that high expectations are usually set and met when a school has effective leadership. Principals have an important role in setting school-wide standards that pave the way for academic improvement (Cotton, 2003). Successful principals are task-oriented, articulate the mission of their schools, and expect their staff to follow their leadership.

THE PRINCIPAL FACTOR

With the assistance from Harvard Professor Roland Fryer, a champion of high expectations, the Houston Independent School District (HISD) has made great gains in recent years. HISD was among four finalists for The Broad Prize for Urban Education in 2012, and it emerged from the pack of the nation's 75 school districts to be named among the finalists again in 2013.

The award is given to the one urban school district that has consistently demonstrated the greatest overall performance and improvement in student achievement while reducing achievement gaps among poor and minority students. To ensure consistency in performance, the latest finalists were determined based on a wide-ranging review of student achievement data from 2008–2009 school year through the 2011–2012 school year.

Professor Fryer, who has been working closely with HISD since 2011, understands the importance of principals. On a practical level, "to instill a culture of high expectations and college access for all students, we started by setting clear expectations for school leadership," Fryer explained in a recent report. "Schools were provided with a rubric for the school and classroom environment and were expected to implement school-parent-student contracts. Specific student performance goals were set for each school, and the principal was held accountable for these goals" (Fryer, 2011).

The role of principals is growing and evolving. They were once expected to focus primarily on managerial duties. Today, effective principals analyze data to drive successful instruction, develop public relations systems to engage and inform the community, and research trends and best practices.

The change is not entirely organic. Much of it has been spurred by recent decisions in Washington to provide billions in School Improvement Grants (SIGs), a carrot designed to turn around the lowest performing schools in the nation under its Race to the Top Initiative.

Funding requests for SIGs are evaluated based on a point system for various categories including annual professional performance review for teachers and principals. Unfortunately, many education analysts believe there are not enough qualified principals to replace those mandated to be fired under school improvement models the federal government says districts must follow to obtain that funding.

For example, one turnaround model for a failed school includes a directive to replace the principal and at least half of the teaching staff. Principals are also likely to lose their jobs under two other models—a consolidation option, which closes schools and transfers students to higher performing institutions and the restart model, which closes schools and reopens them as charters.

Recognizing the need for more "turnaround" principals, many institutions have established training programs to produce school administrators who can lead schools labeled as "failing" under No Child Left Behind. Some train teachers to be principals and others train assistant principals for the top school post. Others train or retrain principals with no more than three years' experience. In addition, others train leaders in other fields to assume school leadership roles.

For example, the University of Virginia has a two-year School Turnaround Specialist Program. Also, the University of Illinois offers a three-year doctoral program under its Urban Education Leadership institute, which includes supervision by principals with successful track record as transformers of urban schools.

VOICES FROM THE FIELD

Dr. Beverly Mathis

Expectations and Effectiveness in School Leadership

As principal at Kermit R. Booker Sr. Elementary, a school in a low-income community in Las Vegas, Beverly Mathis established the notion that when the expectations of teachers were raised, teachers could tend to the major task of raising the standards of students. In 2000, Dr. Mathis won a Milken Educator Award, a leadership citation bestowed by The Milken Family Foundation, which reviews candidates submitted by independent blue-ribbon commissions established by state education departments nationwide. In recognizing Dr. Mathis, the Foundation said: "Following the motto 'It takes a village to raise a child,' . . . Dr. Beverly Mathis has transformed Kermit R. Booker Sr. Elementary School in Las Vegas into a place of strong community, high expectations, and improved student achievement. Dr. Mathis implemented the Gents and Lads Program, which calls upon community

---

members to provide strong male role models to Booker's young African American male students. She has boosted student test scores in part by ensuring that the curriculum is aligned with district frameworks" (Milken Family Foundation, 2000).

Dr. Mathis has received many other awards and honors over the years. For example, in 2000, she won an NAACP Education Award. The same year, Nevada Congresswoman Shelley Berkley presented Dr. Mathis with Congressional Recognition for "Outstanding Achievement and Major Academic Growth and Improvement" at Booker. She was inducted into the Clark County School District's Excellence in Education Hall of Fame in 2009, and the Nevada Association of School Boards named her School Administrator of the Year in 2010.

As principal at Kermit R. Booker Sr. Elementary, Dr. Mathis demonstrated that when the expectations of teachers are raised, teachers could tend to the major task of raising the standards of students. Situated in one of the city's poorer communities and with a student body that is about 82% black, Booker received passing grades in English, math, and other ranking areas from the U.S. Department of Education's No Child Left Behind rating system for the 2010–11 school year, Dr. Mathis' final year as principal.

Principal Beverly Mathis greeting students on the first day of school

Credit: Photographer Tiffany Brown, *Las Vegas Sun*, published August 24, 2009

EFFECTIVE PRINCIPALS

Dr. Mathis, in her work, adopted the following best practices—a code of administrative conduct recognized by the providers of professional development programs for principals.

Effective principals:

- Establish high expectations for all students and, through consistent experiences, make it a part of the school culture and the school district culture.

- Have clear standards of attainable academic and behavioral performance and encourage teachers to hold students to those standards.

- Are approachable and not isolated in the office.

- Ensure that teachers have the resources they need.

- Realize that teachers have to work to maintain an orderly classroom and that principals have to work to maintain an orderly and safe building environment.

- Get to know parents or guardians of children in the school and encourage parental involvement.

- Give adequate evaluative feedback and constructive criticism to teaching and support staff.

- Provide excellent leadership for the curriculum and the instructional staff.

- Ensure that decisions made about student achievement are data driven.

- Provide administrative support that enhances teachers' autonomy and continuing professional development.

Principal Laurie Barron

Smokey Road Middle School, Coweta County, GA.
2013 MetLife/NASSP National Middle Level Principal of the Year

Dr. Barron has served as the Principal of Smokey Road Middle School since 2004. A 16-year educator, Barron taught English at Newnan High School for six years before becoming an assistant Principal at Arnall Middle school and moving to the principalship at Smokey Road. She earned her B.A. from the University of Georgia, her Masters in Administration and Supervision from the State University of West Georgia, and her Specialist and Doctorate degrees in Educational Leadership from the University of Sarasota.

Barron currently serves on the Georgia Partnership for Excellence in Education Partnership Council and is an active member of the Georgia Association of Middle School Principals and the Georgia and National Association of Secondary School Principals, and has recently served on the Governor's Education Advisory Board for Principals. She has also received the Georgia Association of Educational Leaders Outstanding Middle Level Educator Award and the Georgia Association of Middle School Principals Exemplary Leadership Award. Barron is also a National Board Certified teacher, was Newnan High School Teacher of the Year in 1999, and NHS STAR Teacher 2000 and 2001. Smokey Road Middle School is a state of Georgia Title I Distinguished School and a Georgia Association of Secondary School Principals Breakout Middle School. The school has made Adequate Yearly Progress (AYP) for six consecutive years.

WHERE DO WE GO FROM HERE? BUILDING PROFESSIONAL LEADERSHIP CAPACITY

To what extent does exemplary leadership determine whether a district or school is effective? How much of a district or school's impact on student achievement might we attribute to high-level leadership? The research is indisputable. Successful comprehensive school reform and strong leadership are inseparable. Without strong, passionate leaders to initiate, guide, and support change, a reform effort will quickly lose momentum. Leaders must respond to change appropriately and show others the way. Their informed and steady guidance on the challenging journey toward change is essential.

As we face the challenges of transitioning to higher standards while addressing the varied needs of our increasingly diverse student population, successful growth and progress require the support of a strong leadership team with the vision and confidence to initiate and sustain a cultural and tactical shift in instruction.

Schools and districts across the country must realign grade-level expectations, increase the rigor of instruction, assure that curriculum is engaging and meaningful to students, and ensure that all students are able to apply what they know—both on assessments and throughout their academic careers. Successful districts and schools strive to raise student achievement and graduate higher numbers of college- and career-ready students. Experience shows us that these districts abound with models of distributed and shared leadership.

Effective Leadership Qualities

And no surprise: successful school leaders tend to share a common set of qualities, which include the following. Strong leaders

- Possess high expectations and ambitious goals for the success of every student.

- Believe that challenges related to poverty need not be a barrier to achievement.

- Focus continuously on improving teaching and learning supported by exemplary professional development for the entire staff.

- Monitor assessment and track student progress with appropriate support and intervention that responds to the specific needs of individual students.

- Care deeply about the progress and personal development of every student.

- Promote rich opportunities for learning both inside and outside of the classroom.

- Cultivate a range of partnerships particularly with parents, business, and the community to support student achievement.

- Engage in frequent self-evaluation and data analysis with clear strategies for improvement.

Effective organizational leaders, guided by a clearly defined vision and a goal-targeted mission, tackle obstacles, align systems, and build leadership capacity.

Chapter 6

Professional Development: Pathways to Success

It is generally acknowledged that all professional development programs are a way to improve the effectiveness of staff and executives in all fields. However, the effectiveness of specific professional development programs is another issue.

In the field of education, the What Works Clearinghouse, a division of the U.S. Department of Education, identified 1,300 studies as potentially addressing the effect of teacher professional development on student achievement in three key content areas. Attesting to the paucity of rigorous studies that directly examine this link, only nine studies met the What Works Clearinghouse evidence/testing standards. The report on training programs with qualified evaluation standards found that teachers who receive substantial professional development—an average of 49 hours in the nine studies—can boost their students' achievement by about 21 percentile points (Yoon, et al. 2007).

One of the measures of effectiveness is how directly the training relates to the needs of the teacher and to the classroom factors that relate to student achievement. A number of studies have documented the value of focused professional development training. One of the most recent is the 2013 Gates Foundation report on the Measures of Effective Training (MET), a three-year project (Gates, 2013). Funded by the Gates Foundation,

MET is a collaboration involving dozens of independent research teams and nearly 3,000 teacher volunteers in seven U.S. public school districts.

Although the impact of expectations on student achievement is well-documented, there is ample evidence that school districts are not providing the professional development training required to counter the biases that some teachers bring to the classroom. A December 2012 research report by the Education Commission of the States concludes that expectations of many teachers continue to be influenced by factors such as race, ethnicity, and family income levels and that those biases are affecting student academic performance.

The study said negative teacher expectations account for an estimated 5 to 10% of the variance in student achievement and contribute to achievement gaps between white and minority students. This excerpt from the report provides an example of how these attitudes affect teacher reaction and student achievement (Workman, 2012).

> *A teacher might set lower standards for historically low-achieving students or he/she might perceive various students' behaviors differently. A delayed response from a non-minority, more affluent student might be perceived as thoughtful consideration, while the same delayed response from a minority, lower-income student might be considered as a lack of understanding. These differences in teacher behavior convey expectations to students, which can significantly affect their own behavior in ways that impede academic achievement.*

The authors have been involved in a range of professional development training programs that have addressed teacher expectations, studies that have met evaluation standards.

For example, I led a team of consultants who created a professional model for measuring and improving teacher expectations for the Dallas Independent School District, a project involving pre-workshop and post-workshop evaluations. We began by having teachers complete a survey that measured their feelings and attitudes on a range of variables related to successful student achievement: curriculum, principal leadership, impact of student background and expectations, to name a few. The following were among the questions on the form.

- What percent of the pupils in your class do you expect to be reading at grade level at the end of the school year?

- What percent of the pupils in your class do you expect to be at grade level in mathematics at the end of the school year?

- What percent of the pupils in your class do you expect to graduate from high school?

Robert's Recommendations

UNDERSTAND THE VALUE OF EVALUATING PROFESSIONAL DEVELOPMENT TRAINING

In the Dallas Independent School District, the team I led was dedicated to raising the teacher expectations of their students. The team conducted six workshops over a three-day period in October 2010. During the workshops, I defined expectations, emphasizing that they are part of a belief system. I also provided instruction on how to create circumstances and conditions that enable students to meet those higher expectations. For example, I encouraged teachers to (1) give underachieving students more opportunities to respond to questions; and (2) provide verbal praise when they responded correctly. In addition, we stressed the importance of excellent teaching. Ultimately, the teachers participating in the workshop agreed. When we completed the workshop, the teachers were asked to complete a survey on attitudes. Movement in a positive direction was found for eight variables, and all but one of the positive changes [was] strongly statistically significant. Teacher expectations were among the variables that improved.

Beyond expectations, teachers can also be more effective if they have more resources and smaller classrooms. School districts are pushing for improvements in student performance to generate more public support for state and federal funding. They also lobby governments in a bid to obtain the resources they need to improve education. The initiatives and goals vary—smaller classrooms, more technology and innovation, and more early childhood education among them.

Still, school districts need to alter their expectations about the capacity of potential allies in the campaign for more resources. The people on the front lines—teachers and principals—can be their best messengers. However, they cannot fulfill this role without training that empowers them to engage the public.

To this end, we have been providing training that enables teachers and principals to communicate effectively with the media and local communities on school improvement issues. Principals and willing teachers can be trained to help generate the public support schools need. An example of this kind of training is provided in the following section.

PROFESSIONAL DEVELOPMENT: THE POWER OF KNOWLEDGE-SHARING

School principals can meet the higher standards being set for them by sharing best practices. In a trail-blazing project, we provided nine school principals in the Clark County School District (CCSD) with a list of the early warning signs of potential dropouts. We then asked the principals to note how they have addressed those indicators and/or to provide suggestions on how to deal with the signs. The best responses were included in our report *Early Warning Signs of Potential Dropouts: What Can Be Done*, published by CCSD.

Early Warning Signs of a Potential Dropout

- Difficult behavior
- Academic deficiencies
- Attendance problems
- Retention (not promoted)
- Feelings that some teachers or staff members have rejected him or her
- Failing grades in core courses
- Suspensions and expulsions
- Low rates of participation in school activities
- Low self-esteem and low expectations
- Poor personal hygiene
- Third grade student who can't read at first grade level
- Referral to child protective services
- Lack of parental involvement

Other indicators, while equally important, are factors that educators and school administrators rarely address successfully. They include the following:

- Poverty and challenging home lives
- Money as a motivator—a need to earn money
- Gang affiliations and/or interest in gangs
- Single-parent homes—without enough support for the single parent
- Environmental issues—living in deteriorating neighborhoods

THE EXPECTATIONS FACTOR IN PARENTAL INVOLVEMENT

Research shows that parental involvement promotes achievement. To be sure, parental involvement and early childhood education are widely considered the two most important factors in achievement, particularly for children living below the poverty line.

A number of studies that have examined the impact on achievement of different forms or aspects of parental involvement have concluded that parent expectations are the biggest factor. Consider this excerpt from a study published by the Harvard Family Research Project's Family Involvement Research Digests (HFRP 2005):

What is the particular influence of specific aspects of parental involvement?

One of the most vital aspects of this study was its examination of specific components of parental involvement to see which aspects influenced student achievement. Two of the patterns that emerged from the findings were that the facets of parental involvement that required a large investment of time, such as reading and communicating with one's child, and the more subtle aspects of parental involvement, such as parental style and expectations, had a greater impact on student educational outcomes than some of the more demonstrative aspects of parental involvement, such as having household rules, and parental attendance and participation at school functions.

Which aspect of parental involvement has the greatest impact on academic achievement?

The largest effect sizes emerged for parental expectations. The effect sizes for parental style and reading with one's child were smaller than for parental expectations, but they also had very consistent influences across the studies. Parent involvement programs also influenced educational outcomes, although to a lesser degree than preexisting expressions of parental support.

Robert's Recommendations

EARLY CHILDHOOD DEVELOPMENT TIP: READ TO YOUR CHILD

 When I meet with parent groups, they always ask what they can do at home to help their children; of course, my number one tip is "read aloud to your children"—and then, too, talk about the books; engage the children in repeating the words as you say them first. Known as "echo reading," this strategy helps a developing, struggling, or reluctant reader with fluency, new vocabulary, and comprehension.

Tips for Parents on Early Literacy

Children who are read to frequently learn to read more quickly. Plus, reading to children expands their interest in the world around them. So the following are some tips on reading to your child to encourage literacy.

- Read to your child at an early age—even brand new babies benefit from the musical rhythm and physical closeness of a read-aloud on a parent's lap.
- Read to your child at least once a day—multiple times, if at all possible!
- Organize reading times for your child each day—early in the morning, after lunch, or at bedtime.
- Encourage your child to "echo" your words as you read aloud.
- Encourage older children to read to younger children.
- Encourage all family members to take turns reading to children.
- Read aloud with enthusiasm; use your voice to draw children into the story.
- Take your child to the library frequently and at an early age.

The Value of Parental Involvement

Other authorities have stressed the importance of expectations in parental involvement. For example, in an online toolkit called "Collaborating for Success," the Michigan Department of Education (2013) cited factors that make parental engagement effective:

According to research, the most accurate predictor of a student's achievement in school is not income or social status, but the extent to which that student's family is able to:

- *Create a home environment that encourages learning*
- *Communicate high, yet reasonable, expectations for their children's achievement and future careers*

The toolkit also cited another key benefit of parental involvement: "Educators hold higher expectations of students whose parents collaborate with the teacher."

Teachers should find ways to inform all their parents about the value of parental expectations as part of their effort to recruit involvement. However, teachers should understand the full range of parental involvement activities before launching an engagement campaign. Parental involvement is far more than attendance at an open house.

Project Appleseed, an organization that provides guides for parental engagement, has produced a checklist to help teachers and schools create effective involvement programs. Project Appleseed's "Six Slices of Parental Involvement" include the following:

- **Volunteering:** Recruit and organize parent help and support.

- **Parenting:** Help all families establish home environments that support children as engaged, conscientious students.

- **Learning at Home:** Provide information and ideas to families about how to help students at home with homework and other curricular-related activities, decisions, and planning.

- **Decision Making:** Include parents in school decisions, developing parent leaders and representatives.

- **Collaborating With the Community:** Identify and integrate resources and services from the community to strengthen school programs, family practices, and student learning and development.

- **Communicating:** Design more effective forms of school-to-home and home-to-school communications.

Strategies and Tactics for Engaging Parents

The value of higher teacher expectations and higher standards is the subject of much of this book. Expectations are also a factor in parental involvement. If parents understand that their participation is expected, they are more likely to get involved with the school and their child's education.

The first step is to convey those expectations to parents. This could be done, for example, in a letter to all parents at the beginning of the year—a mailed message that discusses the importance of parental involvement. Such a letter could note some of the highlights of parental involvement the previous year—volunteer activities and open house participation, for example. It's important that parents learn that some of their counterparts are very active at the school.

Here is a list of other tips on how to engage parents.

- **Open House Events:** These events should be held at least three times a year. In addition to school tours and parent-teacher discussion forums, teachers could also prepare and distribute academic progress reports for the parents of students who agree to visit the school. In addition, this is an opportunity for teachers to provide their email addresses and (some teachers may feel comfortable also sharing their phone numbers) and to obtain contact information from parents.

- **Breakfast Forums:** Parents are often more willing to meet over meals. Breakfast meetings at the school can be an ideal opportunity to recruit parents for volunteer work.

- **Email:** Many schools make teacher and school email addresses available to parents and encourage their use for day-to-day communication. The email addresses of parents can be obtained at Open House events and via requests that can be made by mail, such as a Welcome Back letter in the fall. This is an extremely important method for communicating with parents. Via email, teachers can promote school events, provide messages on student performance, and set up appointments for one-on-one meetings or phone calls.

- **Phone Calls:** When email communication is established, it becomes much easier to schedule phone calls to parents for a variety of purposes— from recruitment of volunteers to updates on a student's performance. It's important to convey good news as well as concerns about achievement issues during these calls. Also, when these calls are scheduled by email with reference to the nature of the call, it eliminates the shock of a cold call, enabling parents to remain calm and more prepared to engage a teacher.

- **School Websites:** More than 90% U.S. schools have websites. This is a platform for informing and engaging parents on a range of matters—from events at the school to a variety of parental involvement opportunities. Some sites have secure sign-in databases. Such portals make it possible to post teacher assignments, lesson plans, grades, and attendance records. A good site will contain a "feedback" link to encourage parent responses.

- **Newsletters:** With permission from the principal, enterprising teachers can create newsletters on the school website to engage and inform parents. There is still great value, however, in creating old-fashioned printed newsletters that can be mailed because there is no guarantee that a parent will visit a school website.

- **Postcards:** Other forms of "old media" outreach, such as postcard about events, other announcements, and involvement opportunities, are also valuable because there is at least some certainty that parents—via traditional mail service—will receive them.

- **Surveys:** Parents can be energized and involved simply by seeking their ideas and input. This can be done on school websites or by mail via questionnaires. Questionnaires should seek responses to questions relating to the interests, talents, and availability of potential parent volunteers to match their skills and talents with school and classroom needs. Conversely, schools can conduct internal surveys to evaluate their outreach programs for parental involvement.

- **Volunteering:** Recruit and organize parent help and support.

- **Awards:** Announcements of citation opportunities for parental involvement can motivate many parents. By providing and publicizing awards given after some parental service, a teacher can encourage other parents to get involved or expand their involvement. The awards could be as modest as a ribbon, citation letter, or gift sponsored by a business or private fund.

Volunteering Survey

OUR SCHOOL	RATING				
	Not Occurring	Rarely	Occasionally	Frequently	Extensively
Conducts an annual survey to identify interests, talents, and availability of parent volunteers, in order to match their skills/talents with school and classroom needs.	1	2	3	4	5
Provides a parent/family room where volunteers and family members can work, meet, and access resources about parenting, childcare, tutoring, and other things that affect their children.	1	2	3	4	5
Creates flexible volunteering and school events schedules, enabling parents who work to participate.	1	2	3	4	5
Trains volunteers so they use their time productively.	1	2	3	4	5
Recognizes volunteers for their time and efforts.	1	2	3	4	5
Schedules school events at different times during the day and evening so that all families can attend some throughout the year.	1	2	3	4	5

Sources: Northwest Regional Educational Laboratory and National Network of Partnership Schools, Johns Hopkins University (NNPS 2013).

Parental Involvement: An Individualized Approach

When the importance of parental involvement has been communicated and the general strategies for engaging fathers, mothers, and/or guardians have been developed and disseminated, the next step is to create approaches that will engage individual parents and/or guardians. These are guidelines for creating individualized outreach.

- Understand each student's strengths and needs and work with parents to help them determine what they might do at home to support their children's academic success.

- Establish a positive, trusting relationship with your students' parents by celebrating their contributions to the growth and development of their child, no matter how large or small.

- Convey to parents how and when they can reach you to discuss their student's performance in school.

- Showcase successful parent engagement efforts and student learning.

Teachers and principals can find a range of resources to obtain stakeholder support by connecting with Scholastic's team and website dedicated to family and community engagement (FACE). FACE, which has partnerships with many school districts, has created programs that support literacy anywhere a child encounters a caring adult. The program recruits individuals and organizations to provide mentorship support for in-school, after-school, and summer programs.

Marian Wright Edelman

President, Children's Defense Fund

The Value of High Expectations and Parental and Community Support

Marian Wright Edelman, founder and president of the Children's Defense Fund (CDF), has been an advocate for disadvantaged Americans for many decades. Under her leadership, CDF has become the nation's strongest voice for children and families. The Children's Defense Fund's mission is to ensure every child a fair start in life and successful passage to adulthood with the help of caring families and communities.

The important role of families and communities and the value of high expectations are illustrated in her blog on a young man who excelled academically despite the odds.

It Just Takes Everything We're Not Doing Now

"You don't have to be a Black male educator to teach Black students. You just have to love Black male children and believe that they have unlimited potential and opportunity, and they're just as smart and capable as anyone else. And it's hard. Sometimes you have to go the extra mile," said Michael Tubbs, an extraordinary young leader and teacher who is part of the Children's Defense Fund youth leadership development movement. "It takes school, church, neighborhood, government partnerships. It takes relevant curriculum. It takes love. It takes trial and error. It takes being creative. It takes messing up. It takes getting back up. It just takes everything we're not doing now."

Michael Tubbs earned his bachelor's and master's degrees last year from Stanford University, where he became a Truman Scholar, interned at Google and the White House, and was awarded the Dinkelspiel Award, the highest award given to a Stanford undergraduate student. A few months later he became at age 22 the youngest city councilmember in the history of his hometown of Stockton, California, earning more than 60% of the vote. Today, in addition to serving on the City Council, he is an adjunct professor at Stockton's Langston Hughes Academy. He shared lessons from his first year of teaching and many years of mentoring young Black men at a June symposium on "Black Male Teens: Moving to Success in the High School Years" convened by the Educational Testing Service (ETS) and CDF at the National Press Club. This was the third in a series of ETS-CDF symposia on Black males. The first addressed their needs from 0-9; the second the middle school years. A final symposium on the college years is scheduled for June 2014.

Michael's own background might have made him just the kind of Black boy for whom some people would have had very low expectations. He spent his childhood in poverty and was born to a teenage mother and a father who has been incarcerated Michael's entire life. Yet the adults who surrounded him still helped make education a priority for him from the very beginning, aided by the support of some safety net programs that are under siege in budget battles today:

> "Number one, my mom, grandma, and aunt, even though they weren't educated, they valued education and created a space where excellence was a requirement. It was never okay to bring home a B, despite the fact my mom had me at 16. She said, "I don't care what I did. You have to get A's because you can get A's." I would say the second thing . . . a lot of these government entitlement programs under fire are the things that made me who I am, so it was Head Start that the government paid for that put me on the path . . . to reading at an early age. It was people from the church giving me books when I was little that taught me how to read and read at a very high level. It was quality magnet programs in public schools that really pushed me to achieve academically, and then it was Pell grants that helped me get to college. So I think all these government programs we fight for are really important and are really testaments to why I'm on this stage today."

WHERE DO WE GO FROM HERE? ESTABLISHING STANDARDS OF EXCELLENCE

The research is clear: students understand and retain knowledge best when they are able to use and apply it in practical and relevant ways. When students are forced to sit passively and listen to lectures, they may not be doing much more than watching the teacher work. To help teachers move past lectures and create optimal learning experiences for their students, the International Center for Leadership in Education recommends using the Rigor/Relevance Framework. All educators can use the Rigor/Relevance Framework to set their own standards of excellence as well as to plan the objectives they wish to achieve. This versatile framework applies to standards, curriculum, instruction, and assessment.

Rigor/Relevance Framework®

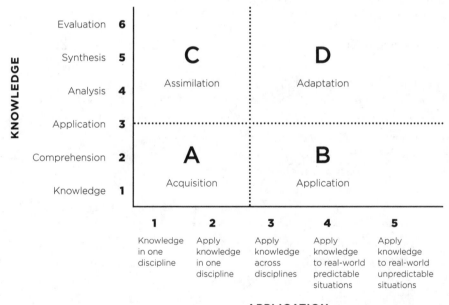

The aim, of course, is to design instruction and develop assessments that measure Quadrant D skills. This enables students not only to gain knowledge, but also to apply and use their skills in the service of inquiry, investigation, and experimentation.

THE COMPREHENSIVE SYSTEM OF LEARNING SUPPORTS

The Comprehensive System of Learning Supports designed by UCLA researchers Howard Adelman and Linda Taylor (2008) is a cohesive and unifying framework that enables all students to succeed and thrive. Adelman and Taylor's work, developed over the course of thirty years in the field, and now extended through a partnership with Scholastic, places student learning and well-being at the center and draws in every component of support—social/emotional, physical, and academic—to create an integrated continuum of coordinated support. The goal is to move away from the fragmented approaches that have marginalized learning supports for students—leading to poor cost effectiveness (up to 25% of school budget used in limited and redundant ways) and counterproductive competition for sparse resources—to one that marshals the full strength and force of the school, family, and community.

The Learning Supports Framework

Based on research that details what schools need in order to effectively address barriers to learning and teaching, the learning supports comprise six categories of classroom and school-wide support, each of which is organized along an integrated, intervention continuum. The six categories are:

- Enhancing regular classroom strategies to enable learning (e.g., improving instruction for students who have become disengaged from learning at school and for those with mild-to-moderate learning and behavior problems)

- Supporting transitions (i.e., assisting students and families as they negotiate school and grade changes and many other transitions)

- Increasing home and school connections

- Responding to and, where feasible, preventing crises

- Increasing community involvement and support (outreach that develops greater community involvement and support, including enhanced use of volunteers)

- Facilitating student and family access to effective services and special assistance as needed

Adelman & Taylor; see: rebuildingforlearning.scholastic.com/

Chapter 7

Innovations for New Outcomes

In January of 2010, President Obama expanded his "Educate to Innovate" campaign for excellence in Science, Technology, Engineering, and Mathematics (STEM) Education.

THE STEM CHALLENGE

A 2008 National Mathematics Advisory Panel report stated that American students lacked the necessary math skills to become engineers and scientists. One of the startling assessments was that American 15-year-olds trailed 23 other industrialized countries in math and that, overall, American students' math achievement scores were "mediocre."

Another discovery was a sharp falloff of math scores as students reached late middle school, where algebra usually begins, and that students who complete Algebra II are more than twice as likely to graduate from college. The concluding recommendation was that U.S. schools need to make algebra skills a top priority since algebra is a gateway to higher-level mathematics courses and successful career paths in science, technology, and engineering, fields that require strong math skills.

However, since those federal findings in 2010, there has been a dramatic growth in awareness of studies that have demonstrated the link between literacy and the capacity to learn math, science, engineering, and technology. Literacy—the ability to read and write—is very important. Indeed, the most important factor determining success in school is a child's ability to read. However, mathematics is the strongest indicator of future enrollment and achievement in college. The two are not mutually exclusive because reading capacity is a pathway to success in math and related studies.

In this chapter, we cite examples of innovation in instruction that incorporates the growing understanding of the relationship between literacy and the capacity to learn math, science, engineering, and technology. The chapter also documents the relationship between project-based learning and achievement. As these relationships become clearer and as schools adopt best practices related to the math-literacy connection and project-based instruction, we can raise our expectations of students' ability to learn—what is for many—daunting study courses.

THE SOLUTION:
HIGH EXPECTATIONS + SUPPORT = STEM SUCCESS

Cleveland: MC² STEM

By integrating project-based learning, real-world internship experiences, and high expectations, a Cleveland, Ohio high school is building a model of achievement in STEM.

MC² (Metropolitan Cleveland Consortium)—or MC² STEM—was created in 2008 through a public-private partnership designed to provide an integrated curriculum informed by real-world experiences. It is part of the Cleveland Metropolitan School District, one of the most economically challenged school districts in the nation, where the average high school graduation rate was just 60% in 2011.

On the other hand, since the MC² STEM opened, nearly 100% of students have graduated, and 84% of the graduates have enrolled in college. The keys to success at the school are an interdisciplinary project-based learning model, internships, and high expectations backed by substantial teaching and tutoring support. High expectations are embedded in the school's core principles. For example, "Master your own path" is a MC² STEM credo.

Students attend classes on the school campus and at sites located at technology companies and universities in the area. Edutopia (2012), an organization that promotes innovation in education, cited the power of expectations in a report on MC² STEM on its website.

Socially, expectations are made plain from day one. Gesturing to the surroundings at the GE Lighting campus, senior Timothy Hatfield says, "This is a busy campus, and very, very strict." With the freshman and sophomore campuses embedded in business sites, there is no running, playing around, or shouting in the hallways. "Every staff member, every employee expects you to be well-behaved and use proper manners," he explains. It is that very requirement of professionalism and maturity that helps foster those same qualities in the students. They see the respect from the adults that accrues to the students who measure up, and it builds a culture of ambition. "If it weren't for those expectations, I wouldn't be where I am today," says Hatfield.

The school's keys to transforming high expectations into achievement are teaching support and project-based learning. The school provides tutors, mentors, and extra study time with teachers. The project-based learning has included exciting challenges, such as building a new audio system for a performance at the Cleveland-based Rock n' Roll Hall of Fame and creating a robot for a citywide robotics competition. In addition, students sometimes get some instruction from experts in STEM-related fields, such as researchers at the NASA Glenn Center, and they are offered internship opportunities to gain firsthand experiences that can help them make career choices.

The value of project-based learning was explained in a 2012 article on the school's website.

CLEVELAND, Ohio—David Boone used to hate science class. Bored hearing his teacher lecture, he'd tune out. Sitting at a desk while a teacher talked at him just didn't really reach a hands-on guy like David, who at age 6 took apart the television set at home and put it back together just so he could see how it worked.

"I like to mess with things," said David, who flourished when he moved to the project-based program at Cleveland's MC²STEM High School. "I like to tinker. I learn better from projects."

David, 18, credits that program both with engaging him more in class and with raising his standards so that he could not accept mediocrity. The result was academic success: He expects to be the salutatorian of his school's first graduating class.

And he was accepted at 22 of the 23 colleges he applied to. Turned down only by his top choice, the Massachusetts Institute of Technology, he's one of the few people who will attend Harvard as a fallback option.

MC² STEM is a magnet school, and teachers at traditional public schools do not have the resources that the Cleveland institution provides. However, teachers of math and science at traditional schools can add some project-based learning to their lesson plans, and they can also bring in engineers and other professionals from STEM-related fields as guest speakers.

Detroit Area Pre-College Engineering Program (DAPCEP)

Expectations are also a driving force at the Detroit Area Pre-College Engineering Program (DAPCEP), which has been preparing and motivating students to pursue higher education and careers in engineering, technology, and medical fields since 1976. The program's faculty members are trained to seek levels of performance from high school-level students that would meet the expectations of potential employers.

In addition to the main components, DAPCEP has a job preparation institute that offers workshops in resume writing, job interviewing, employer expectations, and professional etiquette to prepare students in grades 10–12 for summer employment in the Detroit area.

The program has expanded to include a pilot K–3 program and a program for 4th–6th graders. These programs require participation of parents and guardians in sessions designed to prepare them to be more effective educational partners for their children.

Project-based learning is also central to DAPCEP's approach to STEM education. For example, fifth graders build helicopters, parachutes, and airplanes as they study the principals of air resistance, pressure, and flight. Seventh and eighth graders are introduced to automotive engineering by designing their own cars to bring to market. And high school students work to develop viable alternative energy solutions for the cars of tomorrow. Their target K-12 population is primarily African American and Latino youth. About 50% of the students are female and 30% are from families that are at or below poverty. Finally, the DAPCEP K-3 students who entered the program in 2000 are now entering high school, and many are excelling in STEM and have decided to pursue STEM in college and as a career.

California Mathematics, Engineering, Science Achievement (MESA) Schools Program

The California Mathematics, Engineering, Science Achievement (MESA) Schools Program supports pre-college students throughout the state to excel in math and science and go on to higher education. The program, says the MESA website, aims to develop academic and leadership skills and raise educational expectations.

MESA serves educationally disadvantaged students. Of the participating schools, two-thirds are among the most underperforming in the state. Within the remaining third, MESA directs its services to the most educationally disadvantaged students. MESA delivers its STEM curriculum to student groups in various environments, including MESA classes during the school day, after-school, and on weekends.

Like other successful STEM programs, MESA stresses project-based learning as well as high expectations. For example, MESA works to develop real engineering concepts by using a competitive model where students demonstrate their ability to apply science, technology, engineering and math—from building bridges to constructing mousetrap cars.

MESA has been named as one of the most innovative public programs in the nation by the Ford Foundation and Innovations in American Government, a project of the Kennedy School of Government at Harvard University. It is also is a winner of the Presidential Award for Excellence in Science, Mathematics and Engineering Mentoring.

TECHNOLOGY, EXPECTATIONS, AND AT-RISK STUDENTS

Technology can enhance student engagement and productivity. It also increases the complexity of the tasks that students can perform successfully and raises student motivation (Baker, Gearhart, & Herman, 1994; Dwyer, Ringstaff, & Sandholtz, 1990; Means & Olson, 1995).

Technology can also help students develop positive *cooperative learning* relationships, enabling them to work and learn together as they research topics and create presentations. Moreover, students with special needs may require more coaching in computer-based activities, but they will benefit from the experience of learning with other students.

Traditionally, however, schools have not focused on technology as a means to support engaged learning. When computers are present in schools serving at-risk students, they usually are used for drill-and-practice programs on basic skills rather than as tools to support students in designing their own projects (DeVillar & Faltis, 1991).

Technologies can be used to learn basic skills, but most digital tools have real-world applications that can also help all—including at-risk students—engage in research, design, analysis, composition, and dynamic classroom communication.

One of the leading innovators in high technology applications for curricula is Dr. Elliot Soloway, one of the founders of the Center for Highly Interactive Computing in Education and principal investigator of the Center for Learning Technologies in Urban Schools at the University of Michigan. He has explored how technology will change our expectations of their learning capacities. The excerpt below is from a videotaped interview for the video series *Learning With Technology*, program #2, *Tools for Thinking* (North Central Regional Educational Laboratory, 1995) and *Collaborations in Education: Highly Interactive Computing* (North Central Regional Educational Laboratory, 1995).

"If we follow the naturally mandated guidelines for what classrooms need to look like, we're going to be asking kids to do different kinds of activities than we're asking them to do now. For example, as opposed to reading materials in a book and answering questions at the end of the chapter, what we're going to be asking kids to do is go . . . collect data. We're also going to be asking them to build models of the data that they collect and visualize the data. The only way to do those new sets of activities is to employ technology. Scientists use technology to do those kinds of activities, build models, visualize the data, report on their data, and report on their theories."

ADDING THE ARTS, READING, AND WRITING TO TRANSFORM STEM INTO STREAM

Robert and Michèle Root-Bernstein, the co-authors of *Sparks of Genius: The 13 Thinking Tools of the World's Most Creative People* (Houghton Mifflin, 1999) and *Honey, Mud, Maggots, and Other Medical Marvels* (Houghton Mifflin, 1997), discuss in a March, 2011 National Writing Project (NWP) article the importance of including reading and writing, along with the arts, in training young students to become innovative and successful scientists. They note the movement to modify the STEM acronym (science, technology, engineering, and mathematics) into the STEAM acronym by adding the "arts." They then suggest a further modification by advocating that a more integrative learning approach would accommodate the creation of STREAM by adding "reading."

They note that science educators realize that STEM professionals have benefitted from the arts and visual thinking—e.g., recognizing and forming patterns, modeling, and manipulating skills gained using pens and brushes. Next, they cite that the National Science Foundation and the National Endowment for the Arts have begun formal meetings between the agencies to figure out how to fund research on the importance of teaching at the intersections of Science and the Arts, so that STEAM may expand to STREAM. Below is an excerpt from their NWP article:

Writing, like any other art, teaches the entire range of "tools for thinking" that are required to be creative in any discipline (Root-Bernstein and Root-Bernstein, 1999). To be a lucid writer, one must observe acutely; abstract out the key information; recognize and create patterns; use analogies and metaphors to model in words some reality that takes place in another dimension; translate sensations, feelings, and hunches into clearly communicable forms; and combine all this sensual information into words that create not only understanding but also delight, remorse, anger, desire, or any other human emotion that will drive understanding into action.

Think about it: what we've just described is what a scientist or mathematician does, too.

Moreover, the authors discuss the importance of mastering one's own language, such as the ability to parse and manipulate it in order to master the use of a STEM language—e.g., Algebra 1 with all of its associated symbols and terminology. Contributors to *Journal of Science* (Woodford 1967, Miyake et al., 2010), concluded that mastery of the English language is a prerequisite and an indicator in determining scientific success in STEM careers and academic performance in STEM courses.

In addition, the authors conducted large statistical studies on the hobbies and avocations of the average cohorts of the most prestigious scientists—Nobel laureates, members of the U.S. National Academy of Sciences, and members of the British Royal Society. They discovered that Nobel laureates and the members of the two academies were at least twenty times and—in some cases—up to one hundred times as likely to have a writing avocation compared to other scientists. The authors conclude that turning STEM into STEAM will improve science studies and that integrating more reading and writing studies (STREAM) will help more students excel in the sciences.

VOICES FROM THE FIELD

Kevin K. Green, Ph.D.

Engineer, Educator, and Entrepreneur

The Math-Literacy Connection

Another effective study technique is to have students create a glossary. I discovered through my years of teaching that if students don't understand the language of math, such as knowing certain terms and definitions, this knowledge gap affected their learning the lesson plan for the day. What I saw occurring was that if they did not know a certain term or definition being used, their mind would tend to get filled up with such questions as "What does  that word mean? What is he talking about?" English has suddenly been transformed to some unknown tongue. In my classroom, as I shift from defining a term, I move on to the concept and then a brief explanation and application of the concept. But the students who had not taken the time to review previously taught terms and definitions are mentally caught in the first phase of not understanding the language (Green, K. 2009).

A STREAM School Success Story

One model of STREAM success on the K–6 level is Melrose Elementary, a magnet school in Los Angeles. At Melrose Elementary, children of color comprise more than 60% of the student population. A large percentage of the students are also members of low-income families.

Under the leadership of Melrose Elementary School Principal Bernadette C. Lucas, the school created computer-assisted curricula that requires laptops and the use of Singapore Math, project-based learning, and social networking tools in the instruction of subjects that enhance understanding of subjects related to science, technology, reading, engineering, arts, and math. She also managed the implementation of an impressive robotics program and a partnership with Henson studios to teach students animation.

In 2010, Melrose Elementary students improved 124 points on the State of California's Academic Performance Index, the biggest gains of any public school in the state, including middle and high schools. Under Lucas' leadership, the school also won an Apple Distinguished School award, and 75% of the school's students demonstrated proficiency or advanced skills in math.

In March of 2012, Computer-Using Educators (CUE) Inc. honored Lucas and twelve other outstanding educational technology professionals during its annual conference (Computer-Using Educators Inc., 2012). Lucas received CUE's Site Leader of the Year award, which recognizes a school site principal or assistant principal who has made a noteworthy contribution to promoting educational technology within his or her school. Recipients must demonstrate the following characteristics:

- Strong support for the belief that all students will excel academically
- Exceptional leadership in finding ways that technology benefits teaching and learning
- Building staff morale or the learning environment
- A commitment to educational quality and student achievement
- A commitment to professional growth
- Creativity and innovation in dealing with issues and problems facing education.

Lucas was recently promoted to the Director of the Common Core Technology for the Los Angeles Unified School District.

Bernadette Lucas

Director of the Common Core Technology for the Los Angeles Unified School District

A STREAM Education Leader Speaks

In a Discovery Channel interview, Bernadette Lucas, the award-winning former principal of Melrose Elementary School in Los Angeles, responded to a variety of questions. Some of her responses are provided below. The full transcript can be found at the Discovery Channel website.

What is the future of education?

I'm a very optimistic person, but I'm very concerned about the national state of education. When you look at where we stand internationally, there's cause for great concern. And I think it does go back to the question, "Are we developing skills related to creativity, problem solving, and critical thinking in schools?" And that's where curiosity comes in.

When you look at nations with, right now, better test scores than we have, it's not because they're doing test prep with their kids. I'm sure they're doing that, but their approach is an apprenticeship type of learning, where the kids are engaging with the curriculum as apprentices. They're participating in project-based learning. They're being referred to as scientists in the classroom, instead of students who are learning science. And that's where my concern around American education comes into play. Are we changing our industrial model of education to match where the world is now? I think that's a huge question that we have to answer as a nation.

Should elementary schools promote math and science?

Yes, and that's one of the reasons we decided to bring engineering to the elementary school level so that girls and other underrepresented populations are exposed early. Many organizations and funding sources target middle and high school for engineering and the sciences. I personally believe that that's too late, not just because I'm an elementary educator, but because this elementary school is when the children are starting to think about their possibilities. They're starting to make decisions about who they want to be, what they want to do in life. And so starting as young as kindergarten with engineering, the science, is absolutely critical. So I do have concerns around under-represented populations in science, mathematics, and engineering.

How do you incorporate technology into your curriculum?

We talk about that a lot. And we talk about what social-emotional education has to do with having a school that's so heavy in technology. So we spend a lot of time with social skills, teaching the children social skills, making sure that when they're working on a piece, they're not doing it by themselves. They're working in a collaborative group. They're planning it together. They're creating it together. They're talking and dialoguing about how they're going to roll out the iMovie.

Additionally, when you have a situation like this, with so much technology, you teach the children about "netiquette." You teach them about how to handle what is being given to them. So we create a balanced approach with the children. They're not on the computer all day, for example—maybe 30% of the day, if that.

What will the classroom of the future look like?

I hope that there's always a teacher, a live person, because learning is a social thing. Whether the learning is virtual or face to face, it's a social thing, particularly for young children. As you get older and approach adulthood, I think you can move more and more to an online platform, but children play off the energy of the classroom and the social aspect of it.

I do strongly believe that with online resources more technology is going to come into the classroom, but I think what's going to happen is that teachers and educators are going to have to be more thoughtful and trained in, how to use all of this technology to facilitate a child's education. That's where I think the future lies, is teachers having all of these resources, just like we all do every day with Google and every other resource we have. The question is going to be, how do you manage those resources so that you have a highly effective classroom?

Can a math, science, and technology curriculum include the arts?

I am so glad you asked about that. I don't know if you're familiar with the STEAM movement. Everyone is pretty familiar with the STEM movement. So the STEAM movement, the "A" is for "art" and how we integrate the arts with science, technology, engineering and mathematics.

So many people assume that because [Melrose Elementary is] a math/science/technology magnet [school] that the arts have gone to the wayside. It's the opposite. Our children have theater; they have visual arts; they have dance. And we go to outside organizations. We just established a partnership with Inner City Arts where our children will go to an art space to learn photography and ceramics.

And that cycles back, because when the children are participating in engineering activities, the notion of design and creativity that you learn in art comes into play when they're in their engineering units of study.

Mobile Learning Aids for STEM Education

The list below highlights some of the many ways K–12 educators can leverage the power of the Internet in the classroom, programs that—with the urging of teachers—students can also use at home for supplemental instruction:

- Raspberry Pi is a credit-card-sized single-board computer developed with the intention of promoting the teaching of basic computer science in schools (www.raspberrypi.org/faqs). This capable, tiny computer could be used to create a low-cost, sophisticated tablet that can then be used for presentations, word processing, and watching videos. Most important, it can be used to teach students about computer hardware and computer programming.

- Online, interactive simulations for math and science education from ExploreLearning (www.explorelearning.com) are one of the novel ways of making STEM topics fun and easier to learn. The Texas Science Initiative conducted a meta-analysis of more than 60 research studies that focused on identifying technology-related teaching strategies. Here are some of their key findings on the use of ExploreLearning's Gizmos:

  - ★ Manipulation strategies enable students to experience science by becoming active learners who participate in building their own understanding.

  - ★ Technology-enhanced instruction, including simulations, enables students to manipulate variables and quickly see the results.

  - ★ Inquiry-based learning provides opportunities to analyze data and encourages deep understanding.

  - ★ Manipulation strategies, technology-enhanced instruction, and inquiry-based learning were associated with an average gain of 18-24 percentile points in student achievement.

- The National Science Foundation has numerous programs in STEM education, including some for K-12 students, such as the ITEST Program (itestlrc.edc.org/) that supports The Global Challenge Award ITEST Program. STEM programs have been implemented in some Arizona schools to help students develop higher cognitive skills, enabling them to inquire about and learn techniques used by professionals in fields related to science, technology, engineering, and math.

- Project Lead The Way (PLTW) is a leading provider of STEM education curricular programs to middle and high schools in the United States (www.pltw.org). The national nonprofit organization has over 5,200 programs in more than 4,700 schools in all 50 states. Programs include a high school engineering curriculum called Pathway to Engineering, a high school biomedical sciences program, and a middle school engineering and technology program called Gateway to Technology. PLTW provides the curriculum and the teacher professional development and ongoing support to create transformational programs in schools, districts, and communities. PLTW programs have been endorsed by President Barack Obama and U.S. Secretary of Education Arne Duncan as well as various state, national, and business leaders.

- The Girl Game Company (GGC) is an online resource designed to increase the interest, capacity, and motivation of middle-school girls to pursue courses and careers in information technology (IT). The long-term goal is to increase diversity in the STEM workforce, with a focus on girls and Latinas, and the short-term goals include increasing IT fluency and increasing the appeal of educational pathways to IT careers. The participants design and build computer games and publish and receive feedback in a virtual community. The members of GGC have produced more than 200 games, and the best ones have been posted in the virtual GGC clubhouse at the following URL: www.whyville.net.

- The MIND Research Institute is a national nonprofit organization dedicated to research on learning and the brain and the application of this research to the development of K–12 math education programs. MIND (www.mindresearch. net) has developed a visual, online math-instruction education process that taps into the way we are "wired" to learn. MIND's education programs teach all children—regardless of socio-economic or cultural background—how to think, reason, and create mathematically.

- Khan Academy's math videos on YouTube have become a very popular choice for K–12 students to mine for useful learning videos. The two sites could also be useful to teachers as relevant tools for remediation or supplemental instruction. Khan Academy (www.khanacademy.org) has eclipsed MIT's OpenCourseWare (OCW) in terms of videos viewed and subscribers.

- Homeschoolmath.net provides a comprehensive list of math instruction websites.

- For a superb list of 38 "Best Practice K–12 STEM Education" programs, please visit the following website: www.bayerus.com/msms/web_docs/compendium. pdf. To be included in Bayer Corporation's Compendium of Best Practice K–12 STEM Education Programs, STEM educational programs had to meet the specific criteria (challenging content/curriculum, inquiry-learning environment, defined outcomes and assessment, and sustained commitment and community support).

WHERE DO WE GO FROM HERE? THE POWER OF VOLUMINOUS INDEPENDENT READING

Renowned children's librarian Frances Clark Sayers once famously declared, "I am summoned by books!" More than a decade inside the 21st century, such a declaration might seem quaint. But it's as potent now as it was when Sayers first uttered the words nearly 50 years ago. While today our summons may arrive via digital reader or our smartphones, the essence of books as a gateway to vibrant language, transcendent content, and dimensions beyond our imaginations remains the same as ever. And for that reason, as we consider the skills our students need to survive and thrive in the 21st century, let us understand that we and our students have no more essential, life-enhancing resource than the book. Sometimes, as we think about moving forward, it's best to revisit what has always worked: voluminous independent reading and access to books.

It's not just the book as object but also the scholarly culture that books engender that makes the difference. From a study published in *Research in Social Stratification and Mobility* comes the astonishing information that just the mere presence of books profoundly impacts a child's academic achievement. Conducted over 20 years, Evans, Kelley, Sikorac, and Treimand (2010) surveyed more than 70,000 people across 27 countries and found that:

- Children raised in homes with more than 500 books spent three years longer in school than children whose parents had only a few books. According to the abstract, growing up in a household with 500 or more books is "as great an advantage as having university-educated rather than unschooled parents, and twice the advantage of having a professional rather than an unskilled father" (p. 171).

- The results suggest children whose parents have lots of books are nearly 20% more likely to finish college. Indeed, as a predictor of college graduation, books in the home trump even the education of the parents.

And lest you think that only the privileged with the means to purchase books reap the benefit of books: not so. Even a child who hails from a home with 25 books will, on average, complete two more years of school than would a child from a home without any books at all.

Research from the Progress in International Reading Literacy Study (PIRLS; Mullis & Martin, 2007) reports much of the same. Surveying 215,000 students across 40 countries, PIRLS 2006 was one of the largest international assessments of reading literacy ever undertaken. And results from this study, too, show a similar impact of books in the home.

PIRLS 2006 reinforces on a worldwide basis the well-established finding that children from homes fostering literacy become better readers. Students had higher reading achievement when they were from homes where their parents enjoyed reading and read frequently, books were in abundance, and students were engaged in literacy activities— from alphabet blocks to word games—from an early age (Mullis & Martin, p. 2).

Krashen, Lee, and McQuillan (2010) analyzed the PIRLS data to determine whether a school library can reduce the effect of poverty on reading achievement, and the answer is a resounding yes. The results confirm that variables related to libraries and reading are powerful predictors of reading test scores; indeed, to some extent, access to libraries and books can even overcome the negative challenges of poverty. The researchers describe their methodology and results:

> The impact of the library can be estimated using a multiple regression analysis. The average PIRLS score is 500. PIRLS defines levels as follows: Advanced=625; High=550; Intermediate=475; Low=400. If a country has a PIRLS score of 400, with no children having access to school libraries with more than 500 books, and then takes steps so that all children in the country have access to school libraries with more than 500 books and makes no other changes, the multiple regression analysis predicts that their PIRLS score would improve from 400 to 480, moving them from low to intermediate. The finding that the impact of the school library was nearly as strong as the impact of SES (socioeconomic status) suggests that the library can, at least to some extent, mitigate the effects of low SES on reading.

Books matter so much, in fact, that even a summer away from them has a detrimental impact on achievement. As reported in *USA Today* (Toppo, 2010), by sixth grade, the so-called summer slide may account for 80% of the achievement gap. Pre-eminent literacy researcher Richard Allington explained: "You do that across nine or ten summers, and the next thing you know, you've got almost three years' reading growth lost" (Toppo).

Happily, Allington and cohorts (Toppo, 2010) may have also discovered the secret to preventing the summer slide simply by distributing books to kids. For the last three years, in 17 high-poverty elementary schools in Florida, Allington and colleagues selected more than 850 students to whom, on the last day of the school year, they gave 12 free books, choosing the books from a list the students provided. Three years later, the results are heartening: "Those students who received books had 'significantly higher reading scores, experienced less of a summer slide and read more on their own each summer than the 478 who didn't get books'" (Toppo).

And there is something about owning your own books that seems to make a critical difference. As Rebecca Constantino of the University of California at Irvine and the founder of Access Books, a program that has given away more than one million books, remarked, "It's very powerful when you go to a kid's home and ask him, 'Where's your library?'" (Toppo). If you're an educator who is introducing STEM, STEAM, or STREAM, search for books that promote those concepts and build the essential background information that your students need to thrive inside those programs.

And what happens when students living in high-poverty communities without easy access to books don't read? Communities In Schools, the nation's largest dropout prevention organization, cites statistics that show that nonreaders often drop out of school, and 70% of them face unemployment, government assistance, or cycle in and out of the prison system (Hammond, Linton, Smink, & Drew, 2007). Reading changes lives for the better; for some, reading even saves lives.

Chapter 8

Smartphones: An Emerging Learning Platform

Some of the nation's most effective schools establish high expectations and help students meet them by requiring those who need remedial help to seek it during afterschool sessions. However, because of staff cutbacks in many school districts, teachers often have larger classrooms and don't always have the time for the many students who need additional attention. Moreover, some students cannot attend afterschool sessions because their parents or guardians must provide transportation or escorts for them when the formal school day ends.

Private tutoring is one way to address barriers to afterschool instruction, but in general, and especially as a result of the recession, few families can afford private tutors. Students could possibly get remedial instruction via the Internet and software programs, however, many parents in communities with underperforming schools cannot afford home computers. These impediments are summed up in Figure 8-1.

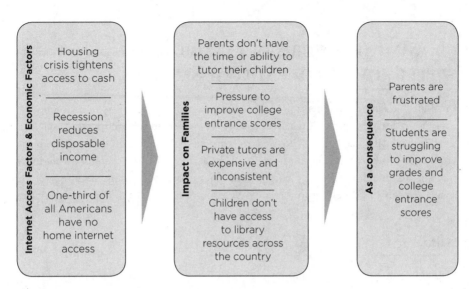

Figure 8-1: Economic and Internet access factors are having an adverse impact on achievement.

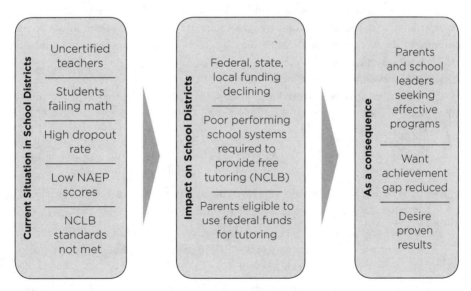

Figure 8-2: American schools and federal mandates are impacting school districts.

GROWING NEED FOR NEW PARADIGMS IN SUPPLEMENTAL EDUCATIONAL SERVICES

In addition to the above-mentioned impediments, many financially strapped school districts are forced to rely on teachers who are not certified to teach math or science. Often, financially challenged school districts also have more underperforming schools. Under the No Child Left Behind Act (NCLB), students at those schools are eligible for tutoring and much of that supplemental education is available online (Figure 8-2). But, again, students in homes without a computer cannot take advantage of those services.

GROWING PAIN OF ACADEMIC FAILURE

Digital technology is expanding our capacity to teach and learn. Increasingly, school districts are expected to take advantage of this technology to enhance instruction for a generation of students that is already tech-oriented. Teachers in higher income communities—with this technology in hand—are empowered and able to raise their standards and expectations accordingly. Educators in low-income communities often cannot set the same standards because they lack comparable technology to leverage the learning environment.

A 2013 Pew survey of Advanced Placement (AP) and National Writing Project (NWP) teachers documents this digital divide (Pew, 2013a). The following are among the findings:

- 70% of teachers working in the highest-income areas say their school does a "good job" providing teachers the resources and favor incorporating digital tools in the classroom, compared with 50% of teachers working in the lowest-income areas.

- 73% of teachers of high-income students receive formal training in this area, compared with 60% of teachers of low-income students.

- 56% of teachers of students from higher-income households say they or their students use tablet computers in the learning process, compared with 37% of teachers of the lowest-income students.

- 52% of teachers of upper and upper-middle income students say their students use smartphones to look up information in class, compared with 35% of teachers of the lowest-income students.

- 39% of AP and NWP teachers of low-income students say their school is "behind the curve" when it comes to effectively using digital tools in the learning process; just 15% of teachers of higher-income students rate their schools poorly in this area.

- 56% of teachers of the lowest-income students say that a lack of resources among students to access digital technologies is a "major challenge" to incorporating more digital tools into their teaching; 21% of teachers of the highest-income students report that problem.

- 33% of teachers of lower income students say their school's rules about classroom cell phone use by students have a major impact on their teaching, compared with 15% of those who teach students from the highest-income households.

SMARTPHONES: A VIABLE ALTERNATIVE TO TRADITIONAL COMPUTERS

According to the Pew Research Center, three-fourths of whites (74%) have high-speed home connections while two-thirds of African Americans (64%) and half of Hispanics (53%) have high-speed connectivity. Collectively, 70% of American adults have a high-speed broadband connection at home via computers, laptops, and tablet computers. However, 91% of US adults have a cell phone. In their report, Pew notes that mobile smartphone technology is bridging the digital divide. Examining the demographics of race and ethnicity, about 74% of black and 68% of Hispanic cell phone owners go online (visit social media sites, send emails and text messages) using their mobile phones, compared with 59% of whites.

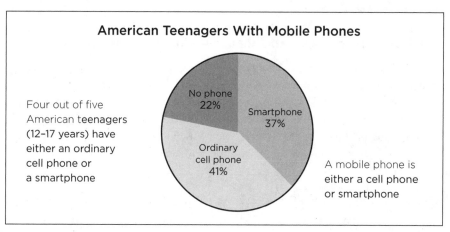

Figure 8-3: Mobile-phone ownership among American teenagers is high.

In another Pew Internet research report (Pew, 2013b), it is stated that 78% or approximately four out of five teenagers (age 12-17) own a mobile phone, and more than one out of three teenagers owns a smartphone (37% of all teenagers). It is important to note that mobile phones are bridging the digital divide, particularly among teens that own smartphones, since there are no differences in ownership of smartphones by race, ethnicity, or income. In fact, black teens and students from poor families eligible Title I federal education funding assistance are more likely to *mostly access* the Internet on their cell phone versus white teens.

A smartphone is cellular telephone that provides Internet access, digital voice, text messaging, e-mail, still and video cameras, web-download capacity for recorded programs, video viewing, and even video chat. Smartphones today are essentially mobile computers. Smartphones also have the capacity to run downloadable software applications. The cell phone market today is dominated by smartphones.

Thus, the rise in the use of smartphones can enable school districts and teachers to provide supplemental education on mobile platforms for students in low-income communities. Ironically, studies have shown that the use of mobile phones and computers for education is miniscule compared to their use for entertainment. This "time-wasting gap" is particularly prevalent in poor communities, where youth heavily use mobile for Internet access and often have parents who are digitally savvy.

Considering the situation, there is an opportunity for teachers to encourage students to use educational cell phone applications to spend more time on learning activities and less time on social networks and entertainment platforms. Edutopia (Edutopia, 2012), the foundation that tracks trends in educational innovation, is a good source for guides on mobile learning.

How Mobile Technology Can Enhance Reading: A Case Study

The report "Pockets of Potential: Using Mobile Technologies to Promote Children's Learning" (Shuler, 2009), conducted by the Joan Ganz Cooney Center at Sesame Workshop, draws on interviews with a cross-section of research, policy, and industry experts to illustrate how mobile technologies such as cell phones, iPod devices, and portable gaming platforms might be more widely used for learning. Two excerpts from the report (below), explain how some educators have adopted mobile technology to improve reading.

Excerpt 1: Escondido Union School District's Project iRead

A group of pilot teachers in Escondido Union School District are exploring the use of iPod devices, GarageBand, and iTunes to improve student reading. Using the iPod's voice memo and a Belkin recorder, students can record and then hear themselves reading, which improves motivation and helps them work on fluency and comprehension.

Teachers can also import student recordings into their iTunes library and create time-stamped digital portfolios (via playlists) that they can use to track progress over time. Data collected from a small group of fourth-graders has found that using iPod devices to practice fluency resulted in more rapid improvement rates compared with a control classroom (www.eusd4kids.org/edtech/iRead.html).

Excerpt 2: JUMP into Reading and Meaning

JUMP focuses on the development, delivery, and evaluation of a supplemental vocabulary instructional game for the Nintendo DS Lite. The curriculum targets low-performing fourth-grade students enrolled in supplemental educational services programs. The JUMP game is a hybrid vocabulary instructional program and role-playing adventure game designed to teach and assess word-learning strategies and to increase the student's vocabulary through an innovative mix of teaching methods, storytelling, and game play. The game involves exploring 10 diverse environments, overcoming robot challenges, completing engaging quests, and solving thought-provoking puzzles.

FIVE WAYS TEACHERS CAN USE TECHNOLOGY TO HELP STUDENTS

In a Brookings report (West & Bleiberg, 2013) titled "Five Ways Teachers Can Use Technology to Help Students," co-authors Darrell West and Joshua Bleiberg contend that the American education system has a remarkable resistance to innovation. Although advances in information technology have revolutionized how people communicate and learn, schools have not effectively adopted digital tools, they say. To take advantage of new technology, teachers must be shown how these tools can empower them and help their students learn. Below are excerpts from their list of five strategies for successful teacher adoption of education technology:

1. **Schools must use technology that empowers teachers**. Teachers rightly reject education technologies that divert their attention from instruction. The best education technologies enable teachers to do more with fewer resources. Communication platforms like Twitter, Facebook, or Tumblr enable dynamic communication with students. Teacher-empowering technologies include mobile apps that grade written student work and provide lesson plan databases. School systems need to aggressively track what works for their teachers and put all other unworkable technologies aside.

2. **Teachers should treat the adoption of technology as part of lesson planning.** One of the major drivers of bad policy is policy churn. New district leaders want to make their mark adopting new policies and jettisoning the old. This constant changing of priorities makes beneficial reforms difficult to implement. Teachers can incorporate technology directly into their practice and insulate their students from the deleterious effects of policy churn. For example, teachers can use Khan Academy (www.khanacademy.org/) or other online resources to improve remediation. Systematic adoption of technology at the classroom levels limits the damage of shifting policy-maker priorities.

3. **Teachers should not fear open-source technologies.** Many people mistakenly believe that education technologies are expensive and complicated to use. Open-source technologies (denoting software for which the original source code is made freely available and may be redistributed and modified) are stable, secure, and compatible with other platforms. Organizations both small and large use open source devices every day. Many businesses use open-source servers for their efficiency and costs savings. They often have large communities that provide high-quality customer support. Best of all, open-source technologies often cost less than proprietary products.

4. **Use online education portfolios to evaluate students.** Educators have known about the benefits of paper-based portfolios for generations. Portfolios allow students to express creativity for difficult to assess subjects. Teachers can choose from a variety of online portfolio providers tailored to the needs of their classroom. They also serve as a platform for students to demonstrate growth. Online portfolios have many advantages over paper-based options because they cost less and allow for more robust outreach. Online portfolios are also amenable to a wider variety of formats including video, music, or other interactive features.

5. **Teachers should embrace the Common Core State Standards.** Common standards make teaching simpler. Teachers have to write lessons that comply with district, state, and national standards. Having a single set of standards eliminates redundancy and conflicting guidelines. Furthermore, universal adoption of common standards will support future technological innovations that aid teachers. From a technical perspective, standards facilitate the development of new technologies. Innovators can focus on developing tools that better serve students rather than solving technical challenges of interoperability created by multiple sets of standards.

The authors conclude that a lack of school financing limits educators' ability to adopt new education technology in many districts. However, they say that teachers in all school districts can help reform and improve education by adopting technologies that are inexpensive and easy to use.

WHERE DO WE GO FROM HERE? AVID READING AND ULTIMATE ADULT SUCCESS

In his book *The Global Achievement Gap: Why Even Our Best Schools Don't Teach the New Survival Skills Our Children Need—and What We Can Do About It*, Tony Wagner (2008) outlined seven survival skills, which he described as the "new basic skills" for work, learning, and citizenship in the 21st century; note that curiosity and imagination (the realm of inquisitiveness and creativity) round out his list:

- Critical Thinking and Problem Solving
- Collaboration Across Networks and Leading by Influence
- Agility and Adaptability
- Initiative and Entrepreneurialism
- Effective Oral and Written Communication
- Assessment and Analysis of Information
- Curiosity and Imagination

The truth is, not one of these skills is beyond the reach of an avid reader. Indeed, these skills define the avid reader. If we consider such well-known intellectuals as Richard Rodriguez, John McWhorter, Calvin Trillin, Melissa Harris-Perry, and Diane Ravitch—they are all from wide-ranging backgrounds and yet they share one obvious propensity: they are readers; indeed, surely voracious readers. As we encourage reading—intensive, extensive reading (Harwayne, 2001)—our students will not only thrive, they will triumph. Consider Thomas Edison, who had little formal schooling but was a "relentless autodidact" and profited from reading books in his father's home library as well as the Detroit public library (Walsh, 2010). Edison's case is consistent with research: Creativity researcher Dean Keith Simonton (1988) concluded that "omnivorous reading in childhood and adolescence correlates positively with ultimate adult success" (p. 111). Multiple studies have shown that avid readers demonstrate both superior literacy development and wide-ranging knowledge across subjects (Krashen, 2004).

Students are reading and writing more than ever and sharing what they read and write through a vast network of social media—and often on their smartphones! In the 21st century, skilled, passionate, habitual, critical readers (Atwell, 2008), aided by caring, professionally informed teachers, will read their way to academic success and, beyond school, into productive lives rich with the promise that reading makes possible.

Chapter 9

Teaching, Learning, and Knowledge Sharing

Creating high expectations for our students begins with knowing our students: What are their strengths? What engages their interests? What learning challenges do they face? Not so long ago, educators relied on cumulative folders to follow student learning trajectories from one grade to the next. The digital age changes everything: Enter Digital Knowledge Sharing. To maximize the power of knowledge sharing in the digital age, we strongly propose that school districts consider creating a collaborative, online, self-paced learning repository where student, class, and teacher information can be stored and accessed via the Internet by all—administrators and parents, too.

Systems and software that can store student performance and be accessed widely can be used to track and improve literacy. Teachers and school administrators should set high standards and then give students the tools to meet those expectations. By creating a repository tool, a school can:

- Encourage teachers to take a more active role in the development of their students at an individual and class level.

- Empower students with additional learning support material.

- Give teachers access to professional development resources.

- Engage and inform parents.

One of the key functions of this online repository might be the ability to upload data into a student's personal online learning "locker." This is an important technological development because it can be used to help address each student's specific academic needs. Here is a brief list of the information that could potentially be deposited into an online repository that would be managed by teachers and administrators:

- Class notes and class/individual assignments
- Additional assignments for students
- Challenging assignments for advanced students
- Remedial assignments for slower students
- Classroom or online tutoring sessions
- Assessments and academic improvement plans for individual students
- Simulation projects for students to further academic understanding
- Online academic progress grade-data entry

Another function of this online repository is the calendar and scheduling feature. This allows information about class and school events to be uploaded and shared. There is a notification feature that allows students and parents to define how often they want to be notified and what method they would prefer for that notification—via email, text message, or audio message sent directly to a phone. With this function, a student can no longer credibly tell a parent that he or she didn't know that an assignment was due or that a Parent/Teacher conference was scheduled. Here is a summary of the capabilities of this feature set:

- Upload and manage class and school schedules.
- Notify the school community of upcoming events using text messages, emails, and voice calls.
- Request meetings with parents (if they have registered).
- Upload online and in-school tutorial session schedules.

The potential of online learning repositories was explored in this 2011 report (Jones, 2011) by former Clark County School District Superintendent Dwight D. Jones: "[The] Clark County School District (CCSD) has assembled thousands of hours of online videos, making it one of the largest repositories of digital media in the nation. CCSD teachers have been creating lessons that are tied to this digital media. Because the media is searchable, teachers in CCSD can enhance their daily instruction by searching the files that are cataloged by subject, grade, and topic to locate the support material and media."

Teachers can make the support material for lessons available, enabling students and parents to view these sessions at a time that is most convenient. Access would be granted by the school's administrative staff based on a one-time registration process. This is especially useful for parents who aren't normally participating in the educational process. Students and teachers would have a different set of functions and information in their respective portals.

Lastly, a Teachers' Online Locker can be created to provide instructors professional development training for instructors. This can include digital tutorials that train teachers on how to improve student achievement. As a part of this service, teachers are encouraged to share their curricula, notes, and individual assessments with their coaches. Here's a brief list of some of the information that teachers can manage for their own development:

- Upload and share curriculum information, schedules, and lesson plans.

- Upload and manage relevant pre-recorded online video sessions for review.

- Manage teacher trainer information—assessments and improvement plans.

Through the Teacher's Online Locker, teachers not only gain a valuable tool to help them with their students, but they continue to use it to manage their own professional development.

KNOWLEDGE SHARING ACROSS SCHOOL DISTRICTS

In the digital age, educators need not limit their search for best practices and knowledge sharing to their school district. On the contrary, considering available technology, stakeholders expect educators to track best practices nationwide to find strategies that will raise the expectations and achievement levels of students in their communities. Here are some reports on this newly emerging frontier of knowledge sharing.

In 2013, the public school districts in Fitchburg, Somerville, Revere, and Chicopee, Massachusetts, received more than $38,000 in state-financed community innovation challenge grants to launch the School StatNet Pilot, a pilot program that enables school districts to obtain and analyze student data across districts. School StatNet will analyze test scores, student demographics, and district spending to improve decision-making on resource allocation to maximize resources and efficiency.

In an article on the Fitchburg Public Schools website (Fitchburg, 2013), Eileen Spinney, the district's technology director said: "We're all urban school districts, so the thought would be that we share similar challenges and be able to share other districts' successes. Hopefully we will see cross-pollination between the districts. We have some district communication using operational data we have now, but we want to increase problem-solving across districts and municipalities."

This addresses a problem cited in a March 11, 2013 article by Katie Ash in the online edition of *Education Week*. In it, she cites the fragmented nature of data-archiving systems in U.S. school districts, the lack of common data storage standards, and the difficulty comparing and contrasting student performance. Without such capacity, it is more difficult for a low-performing school district to identify best practices in other school districts.

Ash quotes Darrel West, who is the vice president and director of governance studies and the founding director of the Center for Technology Innovation at the Brookings Institution, in Washington, DC:

> *It's hard to get machines to talk to one another. A lot of school data are siloed. You may have academic-performance data in one place, administrative data someplace else, and disciplinary data somewhere else. Complying with privacy laws around student data, such as the Family Educational Rights and Privacy Act, or FERPA, also presents challenges. While protecting student information and providing educators with meaningful, timely data are important goals, right now the balance is skewed very much in favor of privacy over data-sharing, so we're not able to get the benefits that would come from integrating information.*

The article notes that the lack of data-sharing capacity has been a problem in Michigan. For example, if a student moves from another Michigan county to Monroe County, the school district in Monroe has been unable to access the student's records. Also, teachers are unable to compare best practices in instructional techniques in various districts within the state. In 2009, the state of Michigan received $11.6 million dollars in a federal grant under the American Recovery and Reinvestment Act to help facilitate information-sharing across districts. The article said the grant provided funding to train teachers on how to interpret and use data from other districts but not much progress was made on facilitating data exchange between districts because the funding was insufficient and did not include money for a dedicated data manager.

There have been similar problems in Texas. However, Texas is now adopting a new statewide data system that will make it easier for teachers or data managers to perform data analysis in an integrated manner.

THE POWER OF BEST PRACTICES: A SHIFT IN EXPECTATIONS

The previous section explored how school districts can use technology to share information that can help boost student achievement. It illustrates a change in attitudes and expectations that can be applied to a variety of problems in education. Specifically, that change is this: school districts and their staffs can no longer resolve major problems in education if they continue to work in silos.

Instead, they must share their insights with other districts and learn the best practices of other districts. A culture of best practices is on the rise. If we are wise and fortunate, this ethos of cooperation will triumph over the old silo-oriented model that emphasized cross-district competition.

That competition-oriented model is based on failed federal government dictates on education reform and/or a failure by school districts to find creative responses to those mandates. Case in point: the No Child Left Behind mandate for a "zero tolerance" approach to school discipline issues.

Zero tolerance has prompted a school district crackdown that has resulted in an explosion of school suspensions and expulsions directed primarily at black and brown male students in poor school districts nationwide. An Aug. 7, 2012 *EdSource* article by John Fensterwald sheds light on the issue.

> African American students are more than three times as likely to be handed out-of-school suspensions as are white children, according to an extensive study released Tuesday by education researchers affiliated with UCLA. Nationwide, one out of six African American students is at risk of suspension every year, compared with one in 14 Hispanic students and one in 20 white students.
>
> "Opportunities Suspended: The Disparate Impact of Disciplinary Exclusion from School" is the latest report (Losen & Gillespie, 2012) to highlight racial and ethnic disparities in student discipline and to call for alternatives to out-of-school suspensions. It includes a *database of suspensions* by race and ethnicity for districts and states.
>
> "The findings in this study are deeply disturbing," wrote Gary Orfield, a professor of education and co-director of the Civil Rights Project at UCLA, in a foreword to the report. "Students who are barely maintaining a connection with their school often are pushed out, as if suspension were a treatment."
>
> Instead of addressing the underlying issues, out-of-school suspension leads to further disaffection and may contribute to the higher dropout rates among students with a disciplinary record. The report does not allege widespread discrimination; however, it says the data "should cast heavy doubt on assumptions that different suspension rates between groups merely reflect differences in behavior." The report cites research in North Carolina that found that African American students were more likely than others to be suspended for first-time infractions including cell phone use, dress code infractions, disruptive behavior, and public displays of affection.

If school districts believe they are to solve the modern school discipline issue with this approach, they are out of step with contemporary practices and the higher expectations of their communities. The school districts that are either addressing this issue or have realistic expectations of dealing with it have formed committees and task-force teams to examine the alternative approaches to traditional discipline that are showing promise.

For example, school districts in Houston, Baltimore, and Washington, DC have adopted the Good Behavior Game (GBG), a team-based classroom behavior management strategy that helps young children master the role of student while developing the discipline needed to sit still, pay attention, and complete their school work.

The creator of GBG works with school districts and communities on all aspects of GBG implementation, including planning, providing training to teachers and local coaches, and monitoring program practices.

Under GBG, children work together to create a positive learning environment by monitoring their own behavior as well as that of their classmates. Teachers use GBG during the school day as a learning strategy that does not compete with instructional time. GBG is built around four core elements that integrate classroom rules, team membership, self-monitoring of behavior, and positive reinforcement to individuals and the group in the form of a game.

Other districts—the Oakland United School District among them—have adopted the Restorative Justice program, a community-based, therapeutic process that addresses youth violence by helping perpetrators understand the roots of their anger and grasp how they have done others harm. This is a high expectations program because it relies on offenders to take a lead role in addressing their behavior and cooperating in discovering the roots. The standards are also high under the GBG model because students are expected to help control classroom behavior.

There are many other alternative program approaches to traditional discipline. In Las Vegas, under the direction of Associate Superintendent Andre Denson and Robert L. Green, a Clark County School District committee of educators and community representatives identified disproportionate suspensions, expulsions, and behavioral school placements with respect to African American and Latino males. The committee also studied a range of alternative approaches to discipline and is producing follow-up reports for action.

To meet community expectations for education—or even raise those standards— more school districts will search to find a best practices model that fits their needs. More broadly, more and more school districts are beginning to realize that they can find solutions to a range of issues by identifying the best practices of what they previously considered "rival" districts.

KNOWLEDGE SHARING AND EDUCATIONAL SOLUTIONS

Whether it's across district lines or within a school district, best practices are disseminated via knowledge-sharing modules. For example, Harvard University's Public Education Leadership Project has a menu on its website dedicated to knowledge-sharing. The section provides portals enabling visitors to provide "perspectives, insights, and strategies" on a range of topics—teacher improvement, school system reform, and resource allocation among them (Harvard Business School 2013).

Knowledge sharing is a practice that raises expectations because when it is part of a school culture, teachers and administrators know they can seek or expect help from colleagues. This notion of knowledge sharing is supported by institutions such as the Carnegie Foundation for the Advancement of Teaching as a cutting-edge approach to addressing urban education issues. Educational institutions in the United Kingdom, too, have been leading the way in exploring knowledge sharing as a means for improving academic achievement. In addition, websites throughout the global educational community have been touting potential knowledge exchanges via the Internet.

However, Internet-based education compendiums are not required to gather, manage, and share knowledge on the local school district level. For example, a project led by some members of this team of authors created a knowledge-sharing project that enabled elementary school principals to share best practice tactics to help ensure that students stay in school.

The nine participating principals are on the front lines of the battle for academic achievement in Clark County. Many of these schools have some of the poorest and most segregated student populations and have been the most academically challenged in the district. Historically, more of the students who have emerged from these elementary schools have been more likely to later drop out as high school students.

The consultants provided the principals with a list of early indicators that a young student will later drop out of school, determinants based on national research. The indicators can be grouped into the following categories: academic performance, student and parent participation and involvement, home and neighborhood environment, difficult behavior and discipline, dangerous and negative motivators, poverty, grade failure, and expectations.

The consultants then asked the nine principals to provide strategies for addressing early warning signs, actions or steps they would take based on their past experience. Knowledge sharing can be valuable because a larger pool of experts can—if their insights are screened and managed—provide more effective solutions than a smaller group. In this case, that meant that—collectively—nine principals know more than any individual principal.

The consultants reviewed the survey form responses of the principals, identified the best responses, and produced a best-practices report that the Clark County School District published and disseminated (Green, White, & Ransaw, 2012). The proposed solutions were thoughtful and often comprehensive in that they included all of the stakeholders in the problem solving. Consider this best practices summary of the solutions to "difficult" student behavior.

Difficult Behavior

Identify the root cause by holding discussions with the student and parents before developing a plan to address behaviors of concern.

Create a school-wide behavior expectations document and ensure that students, parents, and staff understand the rules in the classroom and common areas such as hallways, lunchrooms, playgrounds, and so on. Provide teachers and staff with a standardized form for reporting problems.

Consider forming a committee of older students leaders who can explain school rules at a forum for younger students (grades K–2).

Spotlight Resources

IT'S NOT COMPLICATED!

It's Not Complicated! What I Know for Sure About Helping Our Students of Color Become Successful Readers. (2012). Phyllis C. Hunter, Scholastic.

"Everyone in the community—teachers, administrators, service providers—needs to assume an all-hands-on-deck stance and work together to provide an exemplary academic experience for the community's children." By doing so, Ms. Hunter, an award-winning educational consultant and author, assures us that all students will rise to the occasion. When we believe in them as capable learners and treat them as intellectuals rather than as intellectually challenged, they will apply themselves and succeed.

WHERE DO WE GO FROM HERE?
THE BENEFITS OF KNOWLEDGE SHARING

Power is gained by sharing knowledge—not hoarding it!

On a recent visit to a classroom in Oakland, California, this quote caught our eye. Not so long ago, teachers got a bad rap for keeping their know-how locked up in their classroom closet, guarding their curriculum and lesson plans zealously for fear a colleague might lift and use.

Mercifully, those days are gone; social media and the data sharing capacity of computers are helping to break down barriers that prevent the flow of helpful information and stifle creative collaboration. By sharing your best with a district-wide network—or even across districts—you encourage colleagues to do the same.

Student and teacher privacy are real concerns but while it's imperative that we protect needed confidentiality, there's much to be gained from an open, fluid network. It's always been the case that we can accomplish so much more together than we could ever do alone. And think of the advantages for both families and teachers; knowledge sharing is the easiest and most effective way to keep both informed and current. In New York City, for example, a district knowledge-sharing platform serves both educators and families by facilitating:

- the dissemination of information and high-quality resources that support the city's implementation of the Common Core Learning Standards and the citywide instructional expectations

- the sharing of innovation and expertise citywide

- content sharing, for teachers, and collaboration among colleagues online

Using technology, knowledge sharing helps educators and families learn about and understand district priorities, and supports the selection, capture, and sharing of exemplary instructional practices which will help all students achieve academic success.

Epilogue

A Call to Action

We should not begin with a search for student deficiencies as the explanation for their academic failure or success (Perry, et al., 2003).

As educators, we must never forget that an essential aspect of our job is creating emotionally healthy learning communities, where students feel secure, respected, and confident to take the risks that are necessary for learning—and we accomplish this, in large part, through the language we use. In his seminal *Choice Words: How Our Language Affects Children's Learning* (2004), Peter Johnston notes of teachers, "Talk is the central tool of their trade. With it, they mediate children's activity and experience, and help them make sense of learning, literacy, life and themselves."

What's more, we must never forget that parents send us their children believing that we can help them to succeed (Jackson, 2011). If we don't believe that all our students are capable of productive learning lives; if we regard some of our students as flawed or inadequate then we are engaging in what Valencia (1997) calls *deficit thinking*, a form of blaming the victim. For example, a review of the professional literature over the past 40 years reveals "deficit thinking and terms" used to describe the lifestyle, personal, and classroom behaviors of African American adolescents and other students of color. Such deficit-driven thinking often facilitates low expectation behaviors from teachers and school administrators. It's framed around four central beliefs about the forces driving, or limiting, the academic achievement of students of color:

- the inherent weakness of students of color

- the insurmountable challenges of poverty
- poor parenting
- dysfunctional home life

After exhausting school days, terse exchanges with parents, and challenging IPA meetings, it may be easy to fall into the trap of believing that students of color are failing because of their inherent or environmental inadequacies. But deficit thinking is the opposite of high academic expectations. Holding high expectations for all students is framed by the belief that every student, regardless of ethnicity, socioeconomic background, family history, or test scores has the potential, ability, and desire to excel (Green, 2009).

Enhancing Language

The following list of enhancing words, phrases, and concepts fosters dynamic learning and reflects a growth mindset:

TERMS

Adaptive	Efficacious	Hard working
Bright	Effort-centered not ability-centered	High achieving
Collaborative		Intellectually curious
Communal	Empowered	Proficient
Communicative	Enabled	Resilient
Cool	Engaged learners	Responsible
Creative	Enthusiastic	Rewarding
Critical thinkers	Excellent	Well-behaved
Culturally rich	Focused	Young men of promise
Diverse	Gifted	

PHRASES/CONCEPTS

I Practice	I need more clarity	Sustaining growth
You can	I need help	Praise
I understand	I will get back to you with more clarity	Very good
Yes you can		Hip
I am fearless	I will do research and explain why it truly works	Academic trajectory
I will		Identity safety
I am intelligent		Culturally relevant curriculum
Yes, you can learn _____ (math)	Know the concepts before memorizing the formula	High expectations
I am focused		Encouragement
I need more understanding	Empowerment	Stereotype-free
	Advocacy	Critical engagement

WHERE DO WE GO FROM HERE? EXPECTING THE MOST OF OUR OURSELVES

If we are to help all learners succeed, we must have outstanding instruction, more accountability, innovation, and knowledge-sharing regimes. To achieve these objectives, we must:

1. Raise the standards of teachers and help them transfer these expectations to students.

2. Help teachers, administrators, and parents understand and embrace the new measures and strategies designed to make them more responsible for a new culture of excellence.

3. Encourage educators to adopt innovative thinking that integrates literacy and skills related to math.

4. Encourage educators to replace the silo-oriented, competitive approach to teaching with a zero-sum system of knowledge sharing.

Pathways and resources to these proposed solutions are provided in this book. Educators have access to the codes of conduct that raise expectations and achievement. Stakeholders—school staff, parents, and students—have access to the new accountability standards and engagement strategies in this publication. In addition, we have provided some models of knowledge sharing that can help transform education.

We have drawn upon our collective knowledge and experience and inserted the perspectives, research, and creativity of leading educators. We hope that you will use this resource as a handbook for the high-achievement levels we all seek.

Authors' Bios

Robert L. Green, Ph.D., Dean and Professor Emeritus and Distinguished
Alumnus, Michigan State University, is a scholar and activist on issues related to
urban schools and educational equity. Dr. Green is the author of many books
and reports on urban education issues. Over the past forty years, he has provided
consulting services to more than twenty-five school districts. Dr. Green is currently
working with the Grand Rapids Public Schools in Grand Rapids, Michigan.
In this book, he has applied knowledge from work on behalf of Michigan State
University and school districts in Las Vegas, Dallas, Portland, Detroit, Memphis, and
San Francisco. During his career, he has created staff-development strategies for
teachers and administrators and produced research and initiatives to reform schools,
close the achievement gap, and improve graduation rates. Dr. Green is a leader in
academic performance monitoring and assessment, and he develops strategies to
improve student performance at every level.

George White, M.A., is a communications consultant and policy analyst with
expertise on issues related to education, health, and economic development. He
has produced reports on education for the Center for Educational Improvement
and New America Media, helped Dr. Green develop education research
and training initiatives, and has served foundations, universities, and NGOs
on communications and development issues. Mr. White has helped manage
communications institutes at UCLA and the University of Southern California,
produced reports on community economic development for the Ford Foundation,
and developed strategies to promote initiatives related to health and education
on behalf of The California Wellness Foundation and The Annie. E. Casey
Foundation. In addition, Mr. White has edited research exploring ways to improve
the education, health, and life prospects of young men of color and wrote *A Way
Out*, a public policy solutions report published by the Joint Center for Political
and Economic Studies.

Kevin K. Green, Ph.D., is an electrical engineer, computer vision scientist, and education technology entrepreneur with high school math teaching experience. He has over 23 years of engineering research experience in image and signal processing, remote sensing, and artificial intelligence. He has conducted workshops for math instructors in Las Vegas schools and has a distinguished record as a math teacher. He has also served as a math teacher at high schools in Fairfax County, Virginia, and Montgomery County, Maryland. In 2006, he received a Faculty Achievement Award honoring excellence in teaching from the University of Phoenix, Northern Virginia Campus. Among his publications is "Best Practices on How Teachers Can Instill Confidence and Competence in Math Students," a chapter in *Expectations in Education: Readings on High Expectations, Effective Teaching, and Student Achievement,* edited by Robert L. Green (2009).

Bradley Carl, Ph.D., is the Associate Director for Policy at the Value-Added Research Center (VARC), housed within the Wisconsin Center for Education Research (WCER) at the University of Wisconsin-Madison. Dr. Carl's recent work involves school accountability systems, student growth measures, and educator evaluation and human capital management systems. He has also researched early warning systems to identify students at risk of dropping out and not graduating from high school. He has worked closely with the Milwaukee Public Schools (MPS) to conduct program evaluations and research involving key MPS initiatives and district improvement efforts. Dr. Carl is a frequent presenter at conferences across Wisconsin on school accountability and educator effectiveness, and he provides advice to state-level and district-level leaders on these topics. His work has been cited by the *Milwaukee Journal Sentinel,* the *Wisconsin State Journal,* and *Education Week.*

References

Adelman, H. & Taylor, L. (2008). *Rebuilding for learning: Addressing barriers to learning and teaching and re-engaging students.* New York: Scholastic.

Armendariz, A. L. (2001). The impact of racial prejudice on the socialization of Mexican American students in the public schools. *Equity & Excellence in Education,* 33(3), 59–63.

Ash, K. (1987). Digital learning priorities influence school building design. *Education Week.* March 11. Retrieved from www.edweek.org/ew/articles/2013/03/14/25newlook.h32.html

Baker, E. L., Gearhart, M., & Herman, J. L. (1994). Evaluating the Apple classrooms of tomorrow. In E. L. Baker & H. F. O'Neil, Jr. (Eds.), *Technology assessment in education and training* (pp. 173-198). Hillsdale, NJ: Erlbaum.

Berndt, T. J., & Miller, K. E. (1990). Expectancies, values, and achievement in junior high school. *Journal of Educational Psychology,* 82, 319-326.

Bill & Melinda Gates Foundation (January 8, 2013). Measures of effective teaching project. Available from www.gatesfoundation.org/media-center/press-releases/2013/01/measures-of-effective-teaching-project-releases-final-research-report.

Bromberg, M. & Theokas, C. (2013). *Breaking the glass ceiling of achievement for low-income students and students of color.* Washington, DC: The Education Trust. Retrieved from www.ccrscenter.org/products-resources/resource-database/breaking-glass-ceiling-achievement-low-income-students-and#sthash.owjfpiOo.dpuf

Cepeda, E. (2013). *Lowered student expectations is wrong approach.* Available from lubbockonline.com/editorial-columnists/2013-08-10/cepeda-lowered-student-expectations-wrong-approach.

Chetty, R. Friedman, J. and Rockoff. J. (2011). The long-term impacts of teachers: Teacher value-added and student outcomes in Adulthood NBER Working Paper. No. 17699 December.

Computer-Using Educators Inc. (2012). *CUE honors innovative educational heroes at annual conference.* Available from www.cue.org/awards/2012.

Cotton, K. (2003). *Principals and student achievement.* Alexandria, VA: Association for Supervision and Curriculum Development.

Csikszentmihalyi, M. (1997). Flow and the psychology of discovery and invention. *Harper Perennial,* New York.

Cuban, L. (2013). Meeting and exceeding student expectations of teachers: A way to achieve "good" teaching. Available from larrycuban.wordpress.com/2013/07/14/meeting-and-exceeding-student-expectations-of-teachers-a-way-to-achieve-good-teaching/.

Daggett, W. (2014). Rigor and relevance: Solution briefs from the International Center for Learning. New York: Scholastic.

Danielson, C. (2013). The framework for teaching: Evaluation instrument (2013 Edition). Available from www.danielsongroup.org/article.aspx?page=frameworkforteaching.

DeVillar, R. A. & Faltis, C. J. (1991). *Computers and cultural diversity: Restructuring for school success.* Albany, NY: State University of New York Press.

Discovery Channel. *Experts answer: Bernadette Lucas.* Available from dsc.discovery.com/tv-shows/curiosity/videos/curiosity-expert-bernadette-lucas-videos.htm).

DPI (Wisconsin Department of Public Instruction). 2013. Wisconsin Department of Public Instruction's Principal Evaluation Process Manual. Available from ee.dpi.wi.gov/.

Durkin, D. (1966). *Children who read early.* New York: Teachers College Press.

Dweck, C. S. (2006). *Mindset: The new psychology of success.* New York: Ballantine Books.

Dwyer, D., Ringstaff, C., & Sandholtz, J. (1990). Changes in teachers' beliefs and practices in technology-rich classrooms. *Educational Leadership,* 48(8), 45–52.

Edelman, M. (2013). Huffington Blog post at www.huffingtonpost.com/marian-wright-edelman.

Education Week on the Web (2004, Jan. 14). No child left behind. Available from www.edweek.com/context/topics/issuespage.cfm?id=59.

Education Week on the Web (2013, April 12). The myth of education as the great equalizer. Available from blogs.edweek.org/edweek/top_performers/2013/04/the_myth_of_education_as_the_great_equalizer.html.

Educational Testing Service. (2011). Positioning young black boys for educational success. www.ets.org/Media/Research/pdf/PIC-PNV19n3.pdf.

Edutopia. (2012). How successful careers begin in school. Available from www.edutopia.org/stw-college-career-stem-school.

Evans, M., Kelley, J., Sikorac, J., & Treimand, D. (2010). Family scholarly culture and educational success: Books and schooling in 27 nations. *Research in Social Stratification and Mobility,* 28, 171–197.

Fensterwald, J. (2012). Report pinpoints high-suspension districts. Available from www.edsource.org/today/2012/report-pinpoints-high-suspension-districts/18750#.Ug0zHtLqGOI.

Ferguson, R. F. (2003). Teachers' perceptions and expectations and the black-white test score gap. *Urban Education,* 38(4), 460-507.

Ferguson, R. F. (1998). Teacher perceptions and expectations and the black-white test score gap. In C. Jenks and M. Phillips (Eds.), *The black-white test score gap.* Washington, DC: The Brookings Institution Press.

Fitchburg Public Schools. (2013). State award to help school districts share data. Available from www.sentinelandenterprise.com/ci_22588410/state-award-help-school-districts-share-data.

Fordham, S. (1988). Racelessness as a strategy in black students' school success: Pragmatic strategy or Pyrrhic victory? *Harvard Educational Review,* 58(1), 54-84.

Fryer, R. (2011). Creating "no excuses" (traditional) public schools: Preliminary evidence from an experiment in Houston. NBER Working Paper No. 17494.

Georgetown University. (2011). The college payoff. Available from www9.georgetown.edu/grad/gppi/hpi/cew/pdfs/collegepayoff-complete.pdf.

Goe, L., Holdheide, L, & Miller, T. (2011). *A practical guide to designing comprehensive teacher evaluation systems.* Washington, DC: National Comprehensive Center for Teacher Quality.

Good, T. (1987). Two decades of research on teacher expectations: Findings and future directions. *Journal of Teacher Education.* 38:32. 32-47.

Green, K. (2009). Best practices on how teachers can instill confidences and competence in math students. In R. L. Green (ed.), *Expectations in education: Readings on high expectation, effective teaching, and student achievement.* Columbus, OH: SRA/McGraw-Hill.

Green, R. L. (1977). *The urban challenge—poverty and race.* Chicago: Follett Publishing Co.

Green, R. L. (1987). *Expectations: Research implications on a major dimension of effective schooling.* Cleveland, OH: Cuyahoga Community College.

Green, R. L. (1996). A profile of African American males. In B. W. Austin (ed.) *Repairing the breach.* Dillon, CO: Alpine Guild, Inc.

Green, R. L. (1998a). *Ownership, responsibility, and accountability for student achievement.* Dillon, CO: Alpine Guild, Inc.

Green, R. L. (2002). *An assessment of student achievement in the Dallas Independent School District: Final report.* East Lansing, MI: Author.

Green, R.L. (2009). *Expectations in education: How teacher expectations can increase student achievement and assist in closing the achievement gap.* New York: McGraw Hill.

Green, R. L., White, G., & Ransaw, T. (2012). *Early warning signs of potential dropouts: What can be done.* Las Vegas, NV: Clark County School District.

Harvard Business School (2013). Knowledge

sharing. Available from www.hbs.edu/pelp/knowledge/.

Harvard Family Research Project (2005). Parental involvement and student achievement: A meta-analysis. Available from www.hfrp.org/publications-resources/browse-our-publications/parental-involvement-and-student-achievement-a-meta-analysis.

Hattie, J. (2008). *Visible learning for teachers: Maximizing Impact on learning.* London: Routledge.

Henderson, A., Mapp, K., Johnson, V., & Davies, D. (2007). *Beyond the bake sale: The essential guide to family-school partnerships.* New York: The New Press.

Hill, P. (1998). *Fixing urban schools.* Washington, DC: Brookings Institution Press.

Hunter, P. (2012). *It's not complicated: What I know for sure about helping our students of color succeed as readers.* New York: Scholastic.

ISLLC (Interstate School Leaders Licensure Consortium). (2008). *Educational leadership policy standards.* Available from www.ccsso.org/documents/2008/educational_leadership_policy_standards_2008.pdf.

Jackson, Y. (2011). *Pedagogy of confidence: Inspiring high intellectual performance in urban school.* New York: Teachers College Press.

Johnson, S. L. (2011). An interview with Jawanza Kunjufu. *Journal of African American Males in Education, Leading Educators Series,* 2 (1–2).

Johnston, P. (2004). *Choice words: How our language affects children's language.* Portland, ME: Stenhouse.

Johnston, P. (2013). *Opening minds. Using language to change lives.* Portland, ME: Stenhouse.

Jones, D. (2011). *A look ahead—Phase I: Preliminary reforms report-improving achievement in the Clark County School District.* Available from www.ccsd.net/district/superintendent/resources/pdf/a-look-ahead-05-2011.pdf.

Kane, T. J., McCaffrey, D. F., Miller, T., & Staiger, D. O. (2013). Have we identified effective teachers? Validating measures of effective teaching using random assignment. Accessed May 12, 2013 from www.metproject.org/downloads/MET_Validating_Using_Random_Assignment_Research_Paper.pdf.

Kotlowitz, A. (1991). *There are no children here: The story of two boys growing up in the other America.* New York: Doubleday.

Kozol, J. (1991). *Savage inequalities: Children in America's schools.* New York: Crown.

Krashen, S. (2004). *The power of reading.* Portsmouth, NH: Heinemann.

Kunjufu, J. (2011). Interview in *Journal of African American Males in Education, Leading Educators Series,* 2(1/2). Available from journalofafricanamericanmales.com/wp-content/uploads/downloads/2011/03/Jawanza-Kunjufu2.pdf.

Learning With Technology, Tools for Thinking, and Collaborations in Education: Highly Interactive Computing. (1995). North Central Regional Educational Laboratory: Retrieved from http://www.learningpt.org/

Lippmann, L., Burns, B., & MacArthur, E. (1996). *Urban schools: The challenge of location and poverty* (NCES-184). Washington, DC: U.S. Department of Education, National Center for Education Statistics.

Losen, D., & Gillespie, J. (2012). Opportunities suspended: The disparate impact of disciplinary exclusion from school. Available from civilrightsproject.ucla.edu/resources/projects/center-for-civil-rights-remedies/school-to-prison-folder/federal-reports/upcoming-ccrr-research.

Means, B., & Olson, K. (1995). *Technology's role in education reform: Findings from a national study of innovating schools.* Washington, DC: U.S. Department of Education, Office of Educational Research and Improvement.

Michigan Department of Education (2013). Collaborating for success—parent engagement toolkit. Available from www.michigan.gov/mde/0,4615,7-140-6530_30334_51051-262889--,00.html.

Milken Family Foundation. Milken Educator Awards. Retrieved from milkeneducatorawards.org/

Miyake, A., Kost-Smith, L. E., Finkelstein, N. D., Pollock, S. J., Cohen, G. L. & Ito, T. A. (2010). Reducing the gender achievement gap in college science: A classroom study of values affirmation. *Science* 26 (November 2010): 1234-1237, doi:10.1126/science.1195996.

Moore, W. (2010). *The other Wes Moore: One name, two fates.* New York: Random House.

National Mathematics Advisory Panel Report. (2008). Extracted from www2.ed.gov/about/bdscomm/list/mathpanel/report/final-report.pdf.

Needlman, R., Klass, P., & Zuckerman, B. (2006). A pediatric approach to early literacy. In D. Dickinson, & S. Neuman (Eds). *Handbook of early literacy research*, Vol. 2. New York: Guilford.

Neuman, S. & Celano, D. (2006). Access to print in low-income and middle-income communities: An ecological study of four neighborhoods. *Reading Research Quarterly*, 36, (1) 8–26.

Newman, D. & Smith, R. (1999). Building reality: The social construction of knowledge. Pine Forge Press. Retrieved from: http://www.pineforge.com/newman.

New York Times. (2012). How prisoners make us look good. Available from www.nytimes.com/2012/10/28/sunday-review/how-prisoners-make-data-look-good.html?_r=0.

Noguera, P. (2008). *The trouble with black boys.* New York: John, Wiley & Sons.

Ogbu, J. U. (2003). *Black American students in an affluent suburb: A study of academic disengagement.* Hillsdale, NJ: Lawrence Erlbaum.

Orfield, G. (2009). Reviving the goal of an integrated society: A 21st century challenge. Available from civilrightsproject.ucla.edu/research/k-12-education/integration-and-diversity/reviving-the-goal-of-an-integrated-society-a-21st-century-challenge/orfield-reviving-the-goal-mlk-2009.pdf.

Orfield, G., & Lee, C. (2004). *Brown at 50: King's dream or Plessy's nightmare?* Cambridge, MA: Harvard University.

Perry, T., Steele, C. & Hilliard III, A. (2003). *Young gifted and Black: Promoting high achievement among African-American students.* New York: Beacon Press.

Pew Research Center's Internet & American Life Project. (2013a). How teachers are using technology at home and in their classrooms. Extracted from pewinternet.org/Reports/2013/Teachers-and-technology.

Pew Research Center's Internet & American Life Project. (2013b). Teens and technology 2013. Extracted from www.pewinternet.org/Reports/2013/Teens-and-Tech.aspx.

Redding, S., Murphy, M., & Sheley, P. (Eds). (2011). *Handbook on family and community engagement.* Lincoln, IL: Academic Development Institute.

Rivkin, S., Hanushek, E., & Kain, J. (2005). Teachers, schools, and academic achievement. *Econometrica* 73(2), 417-458.

Rockoff, J. E. (2004). The impact of individual teachers on students' achievement: Evidence from panel data. *American Economic Review,* 94(2), 247-52.

Roosevelt Senior High School. (2013). Extracted from sites.google.com/a/dc.gov/rooseveltshs/.

Root-Bernstein, M. & R. (1993). *Sparks of genius: The 13 thinking tools of the world's most creative people.* New York: Houghton Mifflin.

Rosenthal, R., & Jacobson, L. (1968). *Pygmalion in the classroom.* New York: Holt, Rinehart, & Winston.

Sawicki, J. (2013). Extracted from excellenceboys.uncommonschools.org/.

Shuler, C. (2009). *Pockets of potential: Using mobile technologies to promote children's learning.* New York: The Joan Ganz Cooney Center at Sesame Workshop.

Snow, C. E. & Juel, C. (2005). Teaching children to read: What do we know about how to do it? In M. J. Snowling & C. Hulme (Eds.) *The Science of Reading: A Handbook* (pp. 501-520). London: Blackwell.

Steele, C. M., & Aronson, J. (1995). Stereotype threat and the intellectual test performance of

African Americans. *Journal of Personality and Social Psychology*, 69(5): 797–811.

Steele, C. M. (1997). A threat in the air: How stereotypes shape intellectual identity and performance. *The American Psychologist*, 52(6): 613–629.

Steele, C. M. (1998). Stereotyping and its threat are real. *The American Psychologist,* 53(6): 680–681.

Stipek. D. (2010). In H. Weiss, H. Kreider, M. Lopez & C. Chatman-Nelson (Eds.), *Preparing educators to engage families* (2nd edition), Thousand Oaks CA: Sage Publications, pp. 2–7. 2010.

Taylor, R. D. (1994). Risk and resilience: Contextual influences on the development of African American adolescents. In M. C. Wang & E. W. Gordon (eds.), *Educational resilience in inner-city America: Challenges and prospects.* Hillsdale, NJ: Lawrence Erlbaum Associates, 119–130.

Taylor, R., & Wang, M. C. (eds.). (1997). *Social and emotional adjustment and family relations in ethnic minority families.* Hillsdale, NJ: Lawrence Erlbaum Associates.

Teale, W. H. (1978). Positive environments for learning to read: What studies of early readers tell us. *Journal of Language Arts*, 55(8), 922–932.

Teale, W., Hiebert, E., Chittenden, T. (1987). Assessing young children's development. *The Reading Teacher*, 40 (8), 772–777.

Terrill, M. M., & Mark, D. L. (2000). Preservice teachers' expectations for schools with children of color and second-language learners. *Journal of Teacher Education*, 51(2), 149–155.

Till, F. (2013). Feb. 8, 2013 Executive Summary on Cumberland County Schools for AdvancED (www.advanc-ed.org).

Tough, P. (2012). *How children succeed: Curiosity, grit, and the hidden power of character.* New York: Houghton Mifflin Harcourt.

U.S. Department of Education (1987). *What works: Research about teaching and learning (2nd edition).* Washington, DC.

Valencia, R. (Ed.). (1997). *The evolution of deficit thinking: Educational thought and practice.* Briston, PA: Falmer Press.

Wagner, T. (2008). *The global achievement gap: Why even our best schools don't teach the new survival skills our children need—and what we can do about it.* New York: Basic Books.

Wang, M. C., & Gordon, E. W. (eds.). (1994). *Educational resilience in inner-city America: Challenges and prospects.* Hillsdale, NJ: Lawrence Erlbaum Associates.

West, D., & Bleiberg, J. (2013). Five ways teachers can use technology to help students. Brookings Report available at www.brookings.edu/research/opinions/2013/05/07-teachers-technology-students-education-west-bleiberg).

Wildhagen, T. (2012). "How teachers and schools contribute to racial differences in the realization of academic potential." New York: Teachers College Press.

Wood, D., Kaplan, R., & McLoyd, V. C. (2007). Gender differences in the educational expectations of urban, low-income African American youth: The role of parents and the school. *Journal of Youth and Adolescence*, 36, 417–427.

Woodford, F. P. (1967). Sounder thinking through clearer writing. *Science* 156 (3776): 743–745, doi:10.1126/science.156.3776.743.

Workman, E. (2012). Teacher expectations of students: A self-fulfilling prophecy? *The Progress of Education Reform*, 13(6), 1–7.

Yoon, K. S., Duncan, T., Lee, S. W-Y., Scarloss, B., and Shapley, K. (2007). Reviewing the evidence on how teacher professional development affects student achievement (PDF). *Issues & Answers Report*, REL 2007–No. 033. Washington, DC: U.S. Department of Education, Institute of Education Sciences, National Center for Education Evaluation and Regional Assistance, Regional Educational Laboratory Southwest.